NORDSTROM GUIDE TO MEN'S STYLE

NORDSTROM GUIDE TO MEN'S STYLE

by Tom Julian

Foreword by Pete Nordstrom

CHRONICLE BOOKS
SAN FRANCISCO

IN ALL OF MY YEARS OF COLLABORATION WITH NORDSTROM, I AM CONTINUALLY IMPRESSED BY THE PASSION AND THE EXPERTISE OF THEIR PEOPLE. THANK YOU TO ALL OF OUR NORDSTROM COLLABORATORS—FROM THE MASTER TAILORS TO THE SALESPEOPLE—WHO GENEROUSLY CONTRIBUTED THEIR TIME, EFFORTS, AND INSIGHTS. THIS BOOK WOULD NOT HAVE BEEN POSSIBLE WITHOUT YOU.

—TOM JULIAN

Library of Congress Cataloging-in-Publication Data available.

ISBN 978-0-8118-6836-5

Manufactured in China.

Illustrator: Jonas Bergstrand, Söderberg Agentur
On-Figure Photographer: Koto Bolofo
Stylist: Tim Teehan
Flat and Detail Photographer: James Wojcik
Stylist: Linda Nova
In-Store Photographer: Eric Staudenmaier

10 9 8 7 6 5 4 3 2 1

Chronicle Books LLC
680 Second Street
San Francisco, CA 94107

www.chroniclebooks.com

CONTENTS

AS SOMEONE WHO'S BEEN WORKING FOR NORDSTROM SINCE THE AGE OF 12, I'M A GUY WHO'S EXPECTED TO DRESS LIKE I KNOW WHAT I'M DOING. YOU'D THINK I'D KNOW IT ALL WHEN IT COMES TO GETTING DRESSED, BUT WHAT I'VE LEARNED IS THAT IT'S THE SUBTLE THINGS THAT MAKE A REAL DIFFERENCE IN YOUR APPEARANCE, AND IT'S THE CONFIDENCE THAT YOU GAIN FROM KNOWLEDGE THAT ALLOWS YOU TO PULL IT OFF.

BY **PETE NORDSTROM**
PRESIDENT OF MERCHANDISING
NORDSTROM, INC.

There are fundamental building blocks to dressing well: The pattern on your tie should be bolder than the pattern on your shirt. The color of your socks should match your pants, not your shoes . . . and so on. These aren't mystical secrets intended for a select few. We've been selling menswear for more than forty years, and we share our knowledge in the *Nordstrom Guide to Men's Style* so that you, too, can have access to this information whenever you need it.

At Nordstrom, everything we do is driven by the goal of taking care of our customers, and this book is no exception. We have an ongoing dialogue with our customers, and this style guide is a response to some of the sentiments they've shared with us: Be honest with me. Inspire me. Teach me. Our goal is to give the everyday man a very easy, applicable guide to dressing well. It's not about spending more money on clothing; it's about having the confidence and knowledge to dress right and to be efficient with your purchases.

That's why we turned to popular fashion analyst Tom Julian. Tom is someone Nordstrom has worked with over the years, and he's earned a top industry reputation for working with major fashion designers, covering the runway shows from New York to Milan, and presiding as the fashion authority for the official website of the Academy Awards, Oscar.com.

Does this tie go with this shirt? I still ask myself this question every morning, but I've developed the confidence to make what I think is the right choice. And with our style guide in hand, we hope you will, too.

OVER THE PAST TWO DECADES, I HAVE BEEN WATCHING AND FORECASTING TRENDS IN THE MEN'S MARKET. AS A TREND ANALYST, I TRAVEL FROM TOKYO TO MILAN, LONDON TO LOS ANGELES, RESEARCHING WHAT'S NEW AND WHAT'S NOW. WHAT I'VE FOUND CONSISTENTLY IS THAT TODAY'S GENERATION WANTS A WIDE RANGE OF OPTIONS, FEWER RULES, AND MORE CREATIVITY IN THEIR WARDROBE CHOICES.

A well-dressed man who carries himself with confidence stands out and gets noticed no matter where he is. My hope is that you discover wearable, workable modern essentials that express your individuality no matter where you work or live. Style is inclusive.

Right now we're at a pivotal time in the evolution of men's style. Where once rules dictated what a man should wear and how he should wear it, men are now making their own rules and expressing their personalities through their clothing.

Today stores are embracing the traditions of fine tailoring—from blazers to suits, trousers to neckwear—and allowing men to forge their own paths by customizing fit, finish, and accessories. From skinny ties to cool cuff links, slim suits to rugged blazers, all the options available in stores today allow a man to feel as though his clothing reflects his personality, instead of covering it up.

Our current fashion cycle is like a best-of mix; it combines notable items and ideas from the last few decades into an eclectic mix that can suit anyone. This is a welcome shift from the woefully unrefined days of Casual Friday. Isn't it ironic that a concept that was supposed to make dressing for work easier actually confused us more than the formal dress code we'd been observing for years? All of a sudden, we had so many options that deciding what to wear was overwhelming. Legions of men resorted to what was once the retiree's uniform—khakis and a golf shirt—which is definitely better suited to the golf course than to the office.

But now there's a return to classic American elegance, visible everywhere from Wall Street to Main Street, the Academy Awards to the MTV Video Music Awards. Chances are, whether you choose to wear your tie with an impeccably tailored suit or under a zip-up sweater, you've recently been shopping and noticed the evolution of the men's shopping environment from a utilitarian general store to a true haberdashery.

A haberdashery is a one-stop shop where men can outfit every area of their lives—from work to leisure, dressy to casual. It stocks the basics, sure, but it also offers special items that allow a man to make a look his own. The return of the shopping environment to its roots parallels today's resurgence of classic traditions of masculinity, from hip barbershops to bespoke tailors, cigar bars to shoeshine stands.

When I've talked to men about what makes a shopping experience great, they emphasize feeling comfortable in a setting that makes shopping easy and efficient. They appreciate a salesperson who acts as an adviser, a well-organized sales floor, and instant access to tailoring services.

In my opinion, Nordstrom is the best place to build a smart wardrobe in a comfortable environment. The Nordstrom salesperson can become your fashion confidant—or take a step back when you need some space. And Nordstrom carries a broader range of styles, sizes, and fabrications than other stores, which means I've never headed out on a shopping mission and come back empty-handed.

When you shop for a car, phone, or computer, you identify your needs based on the way you live your life, then you get the facts and make a decision. In this book, we approach clothing the same way. First, you'll discover your style type by answering a few questions about your personality and your habits. Then you'll get everything you need to know about the six essentials of men's tailored clothing, as well as tips related to your style and body type so you can make each item and look your own.

I started my work with Nordstrom because I agreed with their approach to "wardrobing"—outfitting a man for all areas of his life. Nordstrom salespeople are trained to help men create a foundation of quality basics on which they can build a customized wardrobe, and they always have the customer's best interests in mind. After you read this book, you'll understand the terms, rules, and logic used by menswear insiders, so you can articulate your needs and work with a salesperson to meet them. You'll feel empowered by understanding what's right for you. Think of this book as "Nordstrom to go" for men who just don't have all the answers.

I'm acutely aware of the relationship between the way I dress and the way I live. Whether I'm meeting with executives in the clothing industry for a store walk-through or covering Oscar fashion, I need quality wool fabrics that perform. I can be difficult to fit, so I need to try on a range of sizes and brands in order to find jackets that accommodate my broad shoulders without overwhelming my slim frame. I travel two weeks of every month, so I need go-to pieces that never fail me and that look fresh even after a ten-hour flight.

Once you know your specific wardrobe needs as well as I know mine (don't worry, we'll help you identify them), you'll be able to face the world in clothing that reflects the quality, style, comfort, and confidence Nordstrom is known for. Whether you're a million-mile globe-trotter, a weekend coach to a bunch of little globe-trotters—or both—you can craft a style that expresses who you are.

REGARDLESS OF YOUR STYLE, NORDSTROM BELIEVES THAT EVERY MAN SHOULD LOOK GREAT AND FEEL CONFIDENT. THAT'S WHY THE NORDSTROM SHOPPING EXPERIENCE CENTERS AROUND FOUR DISTINCTIVE IDEALS:

QUALITY
It's an unspoken language.
It means taking care of every last detail.
It's true craftsmanship—tailors who take great pride in what they do.
It's only the best materials, collected from around the world.
It's investing in the best—the antidote to disposable fashion.

COMFORT
It's the softest cotton, the warmest wool, the lightest linen.
It's a second skin.
It's freedom.

STYLE
It's like a fingerprint—no two men's are the same.
It's a way to express yourself in a way that everyone can understand.
It's telling the world who you want to be.

CONFIDENCE
It's one less thing to worry about.
It's knowing that you look your best.
It's letting what's inside show through.

Elmer and Everett Nordstrom, 1967

cultural timeline

FROM THE JFK-INSPIRED 1960s TO THE OPEN-SHIRTED 1970s, THE
BIG-SHOULDERED 1980s TO THE MINIMALIST 1990s, NORDSTROM
HAS BEEN OUTFITTING STYLISH MEN FOR FORTY YEARS
(AND PUTTING THEM IN TOP-NOTCH SHOES FOR MORE THAN A
HUNDRED). HERE'S A LOOK BACK AT SOME ICONIC INFLUENCES
ACROSS THE DECADES.

disco inferno

DAVID BOWIE
THE JEAN GENIE
ZIGGY STARDUST

1970

THE
DAY
OF
THE
JACKAL
a novel by
Frederick Forsyth

power-suited

WALL ST

2000

eco-conscious

007

DANIEL CRAIG Broccoli Bond No 6

iPod nano

1960s Mod Squad

From Beatles haircuts and Kennedy posters to peace, love, and rock 'n' roll, the '60s resembled no era before or since. Freedom rocked and youth culture ruled as everything loosened up. Trends originating in Haight-Ashbury, on Abbey Road, and at Bombay bazaars caught on in Peoria and Buffalo. This was the decade when things went global.

1970s Disco Inferno

Disco fiends in three-piece suits strutted their stuff to the Bee Gees while hippie holdouts protested Vietnam—and military haircuts. *Star Wars*, muscle cars, bell-bottoms, and Afros covered the big and small screens, and soul music went mainstream. The shag style was popular in carpeting and in coiffure.

1980s Power-Suited

From Crockett and Tubbs' pastel-colored ensembles on *Miami Vice* to Gordon Gekko's power shoulders in *Wall Street*, the suit ruled the Reagan era. Self-help books and a booming market led members of the "me" decade to believe they could buy their way to the top. All of a sudden, MTV and Apple entered into people's lives.

1990s Virtual World

TV smash *Northern Exposure* and the Seattle grunge music scene put plaid flannel on the backs of every man, woman, and child. Casual Friday consumed the whole workweek, and all of a sudden everyone was in khakis. The dot-com explosion set off a youth quake and sent video-game, flat-screen, and loft sales through the roof. SUVs dominated the highways as the economy boomed.

2000s Eco-Conscious

Bono and George Clooney used their star power to take global issues local. Stock markets and international relations were a study in volatility. A new James Bond brought back classic style, iPods provided the soundtrack for everyone's life, and we witnessed the most significant presidential election of a generation.

WHO...

IT'S PROBABLY NOT HARD TO GET YOU TALKING ABOUT YOUR CAR, YOUR PHONE, YOUR HOME, OR YOUR GOLF CLUBS. FOR SOME REASON, THOUGH, MANY MEN HAVE DIFFICULTY ARTICULATING WHEN ASKED TO DESCRIBE THEIR STYLE. STYLE IS LIKE FINGERPRINTS—NO TWO PEOPLE'S ARE THE SAME. IT'S OUR GOAL TO HELP YOU EXPRESS YOUR PERSONALITY THROUGH YOUR PERSONAL STYLE.

That said, there are certain commonalities that can make fashion decisions easier. So we've come up with four major style types into which most men fall. For the purposes of this book, once you know your style type, you'll be able to quickly put together a wardrobe and set of looks that are right for you.

STYLE

Style can be hard to discuss and define, probably because great style involves a certain degree of effortlessness. But think of it this way: Style is everywhere—in the cars we drive, in the music we listen to, in the phones we use. So when thought of as a series of design choices, not fashion for fashion's sake, style isn't intimidating at all. In fact, many of us derive pleasure from the latest new thing, whether it's an HDTV or a new pair of sneakers—and you can get that same kick from building your wardrobe.

It may be easier to think of style as *life*style—not just the way you approach your clothes, but also the way you approach everything else. Applying your life philosophy to the way you dress integrates your personality into your clothing and enables you to effortlessly adapt the contents of your closet from work to play to weekend.

What's your style? Take the quiz on the next page to find out.

quiz

KNOWING YOUR STYLE TYPE WILL HELP YOU DETERMINE NOT ONLY WHICH CLOTHING ITEMS TO WEAR BUT ALSO, MORE IMPORTANT, HOW TO WEAR THEM. SINCE THERE ARE ONLY SO MANY PIECES IN THE ULTIMATE MAN'S WARDROBE, TRUE STYLE IS DEFINED BY THE LITTLE THINGS: THE SHAPE OF A COLLAR, THE FIT OF AN OXFORD, THE WIDTH OF A TIE. WE'RE HERE TO HELP YOU INTERPRET THOSE DETAILS.

Take this quiz to determine your style type:

1. When I'm not thinking about what to wear, I go for my no-brainers, which are:
    a) A crisply pressed shirt and a pair of classic American or European designer jeans
    b) A soft, rumpled pullover with lived-in khakis
    c) The most current clothes that make me look cool
    d) An unexpected pairing of vintage cardigan, worn-in T-shirt, and skinny pants

2. If I owned a restaurant, it would be:
    a) A prime steak house with a comprehensive wine selection
    b) A classic burger joint, famous for its beers on tap and killer milk shakes
    c) The hippest place in N.Y. or L.A.
    d) An artisanal cheese and wine bar

3. My idea of the perfect vacation is:
    a) Hitting a European city after a long business trip
    b) Jumping in the car and driving to a lakeside retreat
    c) Finding the best beaches—from South Beach to Rio
    d) Going to Iceland to experience the summer solstice

4. The celebrity whose style I most admire is:
    a) George Clooney
    b) Matt Damon
    c) David Beckham
    d) Justin Timberlake

24

5. I like to read:
- a) *Wall Street Journal*
- b) *Sports Illustrated*
- c) *Maxim*
- d) *Interview*

6. The music I'm most likely to listen to is:
- a) Jazz and standards—Count Basie, Louis Armstrong, Frank Sinatra
- b) A mix of rock from Bruce Springsteen to Dave Matthews to the Stones
- c) What's hot—including anything on iTunes' top charts
- d) My DJ friend's private playlist

7. My fantasy car is:
- a) An Aston Martin
- b) A vintage Mustang
- c) A BMW
- d) A Smart Car

8. My friends would describe me as:
- a) The man in charge. The guy who knows which wine to order.
- b) Mr. All-American. I still use my baseball mitt, know how to fix a leaky faucet, and grill a mean steak.
- c) An urban adventurer. I'm always searching for new experiences, whether I'm on a quest to find the coolest gadget—or my hometown's best taco stand.
- d) A trendsetter. It's important to me to stand out from the crowd.

9. On a lazy weekend, I'd enjoy:
- a) Sailing around on a yacht
- b) Watching a football game—from the fifty-yard line
- c) Wine tasting at a great gallery
- d) A fringe festival in my own neighborhood

10. I think of my closet as:
- a) Custom designed and built just for me
- b) The classic walk-in closet that acts as my "general store"
- c) The armory of pieces that make me who I am
- d) My style lab—a place I go to for inspiration

Now add up your answers to determine your style type.
> If you chose mostly *a*'s, your style type is **LUXURY**.
> If you chose mostly *b*'s, you style type is **CLASSIC**.
> If you chose mostly *c*'s, your style type is **CONTEMPORARY**.
> If you chose mostly *d*'s, your style type is **TREND**.

LUXURY

You enjoy being well put together. You appreciate the tradition, skill, and craftsmanship involved in making and wearing tailored clothing. Quality is important to you—you want to build a head-to-toe wardrobe that will last. You want to look good without your clothes shouting, "Look at me!" Your clothing choices portray a quiet confidence.

CLASSIC
Your wardrobe is a collection of great staples. You think about clothes in terms of what they can do for you. You don't want your clothing to get in your way. You appreciate quality, value, and function. You take the basics and make them your own.

CONTEMPORARY

You have a modern approach to fashion, expressing your own personal style through your wardrobe—but you never say anything too off-the-wall. You want to be current but not flashy.

TREND

You like fashion and you're not afraid to admit it. Fashion is just another visual medium—like art or architecture or film—so why not stay on top of things? You are able to make edgy fashion choices look easy, hip, and cool. You're skilled at translating the runway into real life.

NORDSTROM

MOST WOMEN THINK MEN ARE TOTALLY UNSELFCONSCIOUS ABOUT THEIR PHYSIQUES, BUT MOST MEN WOULD (SECRETLY) DISAGREE.

While we're not encouraging self-esteem-blasting fixations here (step off the elliptical and eat some french fries!), it's a good idea to know how to dress your body in order to play up its strengths and play down its weaknesses.

Identify your body type at right. Throughout this book, you'll find tips tailored to your physique. Your body type should in no way limit your fashion choices. It can, in fact, help you hone in on the right ones for you. And if by chance you are a combination of body types, simply combine the characteristics that apply to you.

COMPACT
You waste no space in your closet or in your life. For things to be the right length, you usually have to get them shortened. You may not realize how lucky you are—it's easier to take things in than let them out.

BROAD
You've got a bigger physique, and those few extra pounds you carry are probably around your middle. But bigger can look better with a few considerations and proper selections with regards to silhouette.

ATHLETIC
You've always been a physical guy who believes life is a contact sport. Your arms, calves, and glutes are well developed. You like to lift stuff and it shows.

LANKY
You kept waiting to fill out but never did. While this was annoying in high school, your long, lean body type now enables you to wear pretty much anything you want.

THE SUIT IS IN MANY WAYS A SYMBOL OF MODERN MANHOOD, BUT ITS SIGNIFICANCE GOES WAY BEYOND THE METAPHORICAL. WHETHER A MAN IS 18 OR 81, HE NEEDS A GREAT SUIT IN HIS CLOSET. A SUIT IMPARTS A SENSE OF AUTHORITY, CREDIBILITY, AND CLASS TO ITS WEARER. IT OFFERS STATURE, CONFIDENCE, AND EVEN STRESS RELIEF. YOU WON'T GO WRONG IN THE RIGHT SUIT.

THE RIGHT SUIT CAN TURN AN INTERVIEW INTO A JOB, A LUNCH MEETING INTO A DEAL, MAYBE EVEN A BLIND DATE INTO A MARRIAGE. THE WRONG SUIT CAN RUIN EVERYTHING. THE SUIT USED TO BE THOUGHT OF AS A BACKUP PLAN—IF I NEED IT, IT'S THERE. NOW WE WEAR A SUIT BECAUSE IT REFLECTS WHO WE ARE. WE'RE NOT FORCED TO HAVE ONE, BUT WE WANT ONE ANYWAY. IT'S A SYSTEM THAT HELPS US PERFORM AT OUR HIGHEST LEVEL.

When I put on my favorite suit, I seem to grow a few inches. I know what a suit needs to do for me: soften my shoulders, define my waist, and elongate my torso. That's because my body type is slim, athletic, and compact. Of course, every man looks for different things in a suit. One of my friends wears his suits bold in order to catch every eye—whether he's in Palm Beach or Milan. Another friend, whose supertall stature can overpower a room, needs a subtle look with custom touches so he doesn't stand out.

A good suit offers protection and confidence—it's a sort of urban armor. But wearing a bad suit is like being under attack.

What does it mean to be "that guy in the bad suit"? Something's off, but you're not sure what. What makes a suit good? That's something most of us don't think about, and for good reason—a suit is good when it brings attention to the man in the suit, not to the suit itself. A good suit is free of distractions. It fits its wearer well and lies smooth without wrinkling (unless, of course, it's linen; we'll get to that later). It's made of a comfortable, breathable fabric and leaves its wearer neither too cold nor too warm. It's easy to put on and easy to wear: the ideal go-to garment that makes a guy feel his best.

ANATOMY OF A SUIT

1 INSIDE POCKETS

Inside pockets, which are set into the lining of the jacket, are integral because they're where you put your stuff. Most jackets have one or two, which are cut generously to accommodate things like checkbooks, wallets, and keys. Compartments for iPods, PSPs, and anything else you can think of can be requested for made-to-measure suits.

2 OUTSIDE POCKETS

Pocket alert–limit what you carry in your outside pockets. We know it's tempting and even counterintuitive, but over time, this could affect the shape and lining of your jacket. Most jackets have three outside pockets: a breast pocket, which stays open and accommodates a swanky pocket square (totally optional), and two side pockets. Side pockets come in a variety of styles–see Details (page 46) for more.

3 SLEEVE BUTTONS

While all suit jackets have buttons on their sleeves, some function and some don't. You always have the option of having decorative buttons made operational by a tailor; it's a straightforward process and adds richness to a look. You will usually find functional buttons on higher-end suits. If a jacket off the rack doesn't have buttons on the sleeve, the tailor will provide you with functional buttons at your second fitting.

4 LAPELS

Lapels come in two main types: peaked and notched. Peaked lapels flare out into a point and are the most popular style today. Notched lapels have a V-shaped opening where they meet the collar, as shown at right.

5 LINING

Lining used to coordinate subtly with the color of the suit itself, but these days brightly colored silk linings can be a sign of quality, individuality, and panache. Bold linings signal business on the outside, party on the inside.

While the presence of a Bemberg lining, a silky rayon fabric that absorbs and breathes like cotton, indicates a good-quality suit, a half lining (or even no lining at all) does not mean a suit is of inferior quality. In fact, since more of a suit's interior is visible when it's unlined, sewing quality must often be superior.

DID YOU KNOW?

The seemingly extraneous string going across the shoulder of a new suit is called a "basting thread," and it's a sign of quality–proof that there was handwork done on the suit. It also serves as evidence that the suit has never been worn before. Breaking the thread is like driving a car off the dealer's lot.

FABRIC QUALITY IS WHAT KEEPS YOU COOL OR WARM, WHICHEVER IS DESIRED DEPENDING ON THE SEASON. THE RIGHT FABRIC PREVENTS STRETCHED-OUT KNEES AND ELBOWS AND RESISTS PILLING, EVEN IN THE FACE OF THE DREADED CHAFE. THE WRONG FABRIC CAN LEAVE YOU LOOKING LIKE YOU HAND WASHED YOUR SUIT AND HUNG IT IN THE BATHROOM TO DRY. SEE BELOW FOR THE SIX MOST COMMON SUIT FABRICS.

WOOL

Wool is the most widely used textile in the world, probably because it is the plywood of fabric—you can make almost anything out of it. Because of the structure of its fibers, wool has a unique insulating quality and excellent elasticity (which means that, even if wrinkled and stretched, the fabric will recover its original shape). Because its fibers have a thin outer membrane, wool is naturally water-resistant. But, almost paradoxically, it's also very absorbent. This means it wicks moisture away from the body while preventing outside moisture from penetrating.

WOOL GABARDINE

Wool gabardine is a tightly woven fabric that is ribbed diagonally on one side and smooth on the other, with a slight sheen.

WOOL CREPE

Wool crepe is a "broken" twill, which means that its yarns are highly twisted to provide a slightly pebbled texture. Note that most wool weaves can be applied to other fibers as well, hence "silk crepe" or "cotton gabardine."

Wool comes in many grades, which are determined by the fineness and length of the fibers. The finer a fiber, the higher its grade. For example, a wool graded super 140s is made from finer fibers than one graded super 100s. The higher the grade, the softer and lighter the fabric. Super 100s to 140s are considered performance wools—they can go from the office to drinks to dinner without wrinkling or losing their shape. Performance wools are also great for travel because they do very well in a suitcase.

STYLE TIP:
Before you purchase a suit, turn the jacket and pants inside out so you can examine the sewing quality and look for fine linings on both pieces.

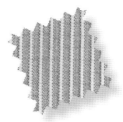

COTTON

Cotton is durable and breathable. A brushed-cotton suit provides a polished look for sultry days and is as comfortable as a pair of khakis and a jean jacket. Cotton suits may be worn from spring through fall, and soon enough we may be sporting them year-round.

Cotton suits are easy to wear as separates—throw the jacket on with a linen shirt and your favorite jeans, or wear the trousers with a casual polo. Just remember: Always clean both parts of a cotton suit together, whether or not both pieces need it. This will help keep the color uniform by allowing the pieces to fade at the same rate.

LINEN

Linen is traditionally made from the flax plant, but in recent years the term "linen" has also been used to refer to fabrics made from hemp and cotton. What makes linen fibers unique is that they're fine but also somewhat irregular, which results in a slightly nubby texture. Linen is more than twice as strong as cotton and highly absorbent. It is also famously wrinkly, hence it's an excellent choice for travel and those with an ironing-board aversion (just blame those rumples on the fabric).

SEERSUCKER

Seersucker is another casual suit fabric. Its pastel-and-white striped pattern has been a classic choice for summer since British colonial days (it originated in the Middle East), but it's also a perfect representation of today's preppy-punk aesthetic and a new take on classic American dressing that's Gatsby-meets-MTV. Like white shoes and SPF 50, seersucker is meant for the lazy, hazy days of summer. We know it's hard to keep a suit looking crisp when it's ninety-five degrees outside, but don't forgo buying a summer suit because you're afraid of it wrinkling. Wrinkles are part of this relaxed look's charm.

THE REASON MENSWEAR PATTERNS TEND TO BE SO SUBTLE AND PRECISE IS THAT THEY ARE WOVEN INTO THE FABRIC RATHER THAN PRINTED ON IT. FOLLOWING ARE SOME OF THE MOST COMMON PATTERNS, ORGANIZED (HIGHLY UNSCIENTIFICALLY) BY POPULARITY.

PINSTRIPES
These superfine stripes run vertically down a fabric. They can add height to a compact man.

CHALK STRIPES
This stripe looks as though it was drawn with a very well-sharpened piece of . . . chalk.

HERRINGBONE
Threads woven in opposite diagonals form a chevron pattern.

TWEED
Tweed has a rough texture that results from different sorts of yarns being woven together.

GLEN PLAID
This pattern has a "broken" (irregular) check, usually with a base of black-and-white intersecting stripes and often punctuated with thin lines of color.

BIRD'S EYE PLAID
A diamond weave on a textured wool fabric.

DID YOU KNOW?
The reason sleeves had buttons in the first place was to enable a man to wash his hands without removing his jacket, which was considered improper.

FINDING A JACKET THAT FITS PROPERLY IS A BIT LIKE MEETING YOUR TRUE LOVE—YOU JUST KNOW. OKAY, MAYBE THE PROCESS ISN'T QUITE SO ROMANTIC, BUT WHEN YOU PUT ON A JACKET THAT REALLY FITS, YOU SHOULD FEEL A SENSATION OF LIGHTNESS.

This feeling describes the balance of the jacket, and it means that your body is sitting right in the middle of the jacket's construction, exactly where the designer intended. When a jacket isn't properly balanced, it can shift forward or backward, or feel heavy on your shoulders and neck. This does not mean the coat isn't well made; it just means that it isn't the best choice for your body type.

It's important to understand that while some things about a jacket can be "fixed" in alterations—sleeve length and button placement, for example—the balance of a jacket cannot be reengineered, even by the most expert of tailors. Altering seams in the collar, chest, and armhole areas should be avoided whenever possible, since fixing one fit element may throw another off-balance; the cycle becomes endless. Another element that can be difficult to change is length. Shortening a jacket can throw its proportions off-kilter, bringing the hem too close to the pockets and making the wearer appear, paradoxically, shorter. Lengthening a jacket is virtually impossible.

Try on as many jackets as it takes for you to find the right one. With all the options out there, you'll have lots to choose from. Nordstrom offers a variety of choices for every style and body type, so don't be afraid to experiment, and consider trying on all the options the salesperson presents—you never know which one will click. In the fitting room, be sure to stock the inside pockets with whatever you usually carry around (your wallet, glasses, phone, or PDA) and check to see that the suit hangs properly when weighted. When you're wearing your perfect jacket, you'll forget it's there.

CLASSIC

A classic fit is so called because it's been around forever. Its relaxed shape means an easy jacket with lots of room under the arms and through the middle. Classic fits are sometimes referred to as "American" because they are inspired by classic Ivy League looks from the 1940s. A classic fit means a straight jacket with a classic lapel, low armholes, and a center vent. It has a natural shoulder and, because it's roomy, requires less tailoring than its sleeker cousins.

Best for: All body types

MODERN

Modern silhouettes fit close to the body but never feel restrictive. The modern jacket is slightly shorter than the classic one, with a higher armhole and a softer shoulder. These days "British" can function as a synonym for modern; this is because the close fit derives from classic tailoring techniques pioneered on London's Savile Row. The modern fit has squarer shoulders, a nipped-in waist with side vents, and a narrower lapel.

Best for: Lanky, Compact

Whatever the silhouette, familiarize yourself with the rules on the next page to ensure the proper fit of all your jacket parts.

STYLE TIP:
Sometimes you'll hear a suit fit referred to as "athletic" or "international." This means it is full in the shoulders and narrow at the waist, like an athlete's physique.

You're probably thinking, "How am I supposed to know when I've found my perfect jacket? They all feel fine to me." Here are a few crucial points to keep in mind that will help even the least self-aware guy determine whether a jacket fits him.

1 COLLAR AND BACK

The jacket collar should hug your neck about halfway up your shirt collar and lie smoothly across your upper back without any bubbling or rippling. A long, horizontal ripple means the jacket is too big. If a jacket's collar seems to want to pull away from your neck, it doesn't like you. Take the hint and put the jacket back on its hanger.

2 CHEST AND WAIST

The jacket should be easy to button. You don't want to see any puckering around the holes when they're fastened and the chest should lie smoothly without gaping. You should be able to sit down with your jacket fastened and there should be 3 to 5 inches of play between your body and the jacket's top button. Be sure the jacket doesn't cling in any unflattering spots and check that its vents lie flat—if they strain open, the jacket is too tight.

3 SHOULDERS

We're not going for a linebacker look here, or anything reminiscent of Gordon Gekko in *Wall Street*. Shoulder pads can create a strong, solid line and contribute to a jacket's comfort, but it's crucial they not be too big. The shoulder pads in a jacket should match up with your shoulders. The shoulders are the base of the garment. If it doesn't fit you point to point, it's not the right jacket.

4 SLEEVES

In terms of length, sleeves should allow about ½ inch of shirt to show at the wrist when the arm is relaxed—roughly the same margin as the bit of collar that shows on the back of the neck. Jacket sleeves should end where wrist and hand meet. Check to see that left and right sleeves hit in the same place; many men have arms of slightly different lengths, and this needs to be accounted for in alterations. For maximum comfort and mobility, be sure the sleeves are full toward the shoulder to give those biceps room to breathe.

5 ARMHOLE

The armhole should allow considerable range of motion. Just because something is formal doesn't mean it shouldn't be comfortable.

6 COAT LENGTH

The general rule is for the jacket to just cover your entire seat. Another yardstick relates coat length to arm length: The hem of the jacket should end near the tip of your thumb when your arm is relaxed in order to avoid a gorilla-esque effect. And here is perhaps the most important thing to be honest about when checking the length of your coat: your posture. You likely stand tall and proud as you check yourself out in the fitting room mirror but slouch a bit in your daily life.

THE DETAILS ON A SUIT CAN BE VERY UNNOTICEABLE, BUT THEY STILL PROJECT A DISTINCT EDGE FOR THE WEARER. BUTTONS, FLAPS, AND VENTS ARE WORTH NOTICING.

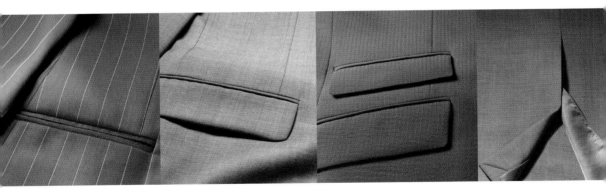

BESOM POCKETS
Set into the jacket like a slit, this pocket has a plain opening.

FLAP POCKETS
These are besom pockets covered by flaps.

A TICKET POCKET
This is a narrow, single pocket set above one flap pocket. Made-to-measure suits often have a ticket pocket. The presence of such a novelty is a sign of quality.

VENTS
A vent allows for both a tailored fit and easy movement. A **center vent** is traditional; two **side vents** are more modern and keep the jacket's silhouette sleek.

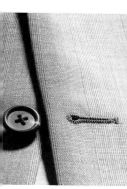

ONE-BUTTON JACKET
This style reflects where fashion has been heading during recent years. It looks great in peaked-lapel suits and is commonly found in tuxedos and among less formal offerings in the modern silhouette.

Best for: Lanky, Athletic, Compact

TWO-BUTTON JACKET
The most common jacket, it's flattering on pretty much anyone because its V points the eye to the slimmest point of a man's waist (the area near the top button).

Best for: All body types

THREE-BUTTON JACKET
The most traditional jacket is also universally flattering. It is derived from English riding styles, so this jacket allows for movement.

Best for: All body types

KISSING BUTTONS
This refers to high-quality sleeve buttons slightly overlapping one another.

HOW YOU CHOOSE TO WEAR A SUIT IS AS IMPORTANT AS THE SUIT ITSELF. THE WAY A LOOK IS "STYLED"—MEANING, WHICH OTHER ITEMS YOU CHOOSE TO PAIR WITH YOUR SUIT—DETERMINES THE VIBE YOU'RE SENDING. THROUGHOUT THIS BOOK, YOU'LL FIND WARDROBE STAPLES TO COMPLEMENT YOUR STYLE TYPE—WHICHEVER ONE YOU ARE.

LUXURY
An Italian suit always offers the ultimate in craftsmanship and luxurious fabrics. A bold shirt and tie give it an impeccable finish.

CLASSIC
A notch lapel and two-button jacket are reliable and true. An updated striped tie keeps everything in the comfort zone.

CONTEMPORARY
A jacket in a high-shine fabric with a high shoulder and a tick pocket feels totally new worn with a small-collared shirt and narrow necktie.

:ND
ader shoulder, bolder
s, and narrow waist create
re exaggerated silhouette.
ge-looking shoes and
er pants give it an edge.

SPRING SUITS

A LIGHTWEIGHT PERFORMANCE WOOL SUIT IS YOUR SPRING STAPLE. AND ALTHOUGH THESE SUITS LOOK SIMILAR AT FIRST GLANCE, EACH CONVEYS ITS OWN MESSAGE. A MATTER OF INCHES DIFFERENTIATES THEM, WHETHER AT THE SHOULDER, THE LAPEL, OR THE WAIST. CHECK OUT THE LOOKS WE CREATED ESPECIALLY FOR EACH STYLE TYPE AND USE THEM AS INSPIRATION TO BUILD YOUR OWN.

CLASSIC

Classic need not be boring. Pinstripes, side vents, light shoes, and a pocket square make this look perfect for a special occasion.

LUXURY

This look is icy-cool. A neat patterned pink tie and white pocket square keep things clean but beyond simple.

TREND

To give a suit an edge, style it with a crinkle white oxford shirt and white canvas shoes. Layering a vest underneath makes a hip statement.

CONTEMPORARY

Go a bit more body-conscious with a narrow lapel, waist, and trouser. Try a contrasting white spread-collar shirt for sophistication.

FALL SUITS

THERE'S MORE THAN ONE MAN IN THE GREY (FLANNEL) SUIT. A GREY SUIT IS THE PERFECT NEUTRAL PALETTE ON WHICH TO BUILD A TRULY INDIVIDUAL LOOK. AND A MEDIUM-WEIGHT PERFORMANCE WOOL CAN TAKE YOU THROUGH ALMOST ANY DAY OF THE YEAR.

LUXURY

Combining blues and browns with grey is unexpected and dashing. A blue spread-collar shirt and dark brown tie create a strong focal point.

CLASSIC

When you don't like competing patterns, stick with stripes on both your suit and tie. A black belt and shoes give the look function and wearability.

CONTEMPORARY

Use the pinstripe color (here, blue) to inspire accents in your shirt and socks. A high-shine tie and loafer create a dressy look.

TREND

The cardigan and Chelsea boot give this look a dressed-down feeling, while the dark shirt and tie give it a downtown edge.

LUXURY
Project a powerful stance with a mix of black and white.

CLASSIC
Update your look with a two-button jacket, a trim pant, and a narrow tie.

CONTEMPORARY
Go lean and layered with a three-piece suit and linear accessories.

TREND
Subvert everyone's expectations with a wide, padded shoulder and broad lapels.

ASK THE NORDSTROM TAILOR

What is the gorge and why do I need to know?
The gorge is the distance between the shoulders of a suit and its first button. A measurement relevant both to fit and to style, the gorge determines how much room your chest and shoulders have in a jacket. Stylewise, it determines how much of your tie and shirt show. Because fit and style combine to form flattery, slim men will benefit from a deeper gorge, as this will show more shirt and make them appear broader. Larger men look good with a shallower gorge, as this gives their midsection more coverage.

How many size options do I have when shopping at a store like Nordstrom, whether I'm a long or a short? Will my size vary across brands?
You have more than thirty sizes to select from at Nordstrom stores. With so much out there, be sure to try on at least two sizes per brand. Different brands are cut differently; some are more generous, others more spare. So many people are hung up on size, but the number is unimportant—different models will fit different ways.

Commissioning a made-to-measure suit entails what exactly? How much more expensive is it than buying something off the rack?
To begin, a salesperson will guide you through the ordering process. A tailor will then take your measurements, which will be applied to the existing suit pattern at the factory. There's not a single guy who won't benefit from a made-to-measure suit. Sure, perfectly proportioned men can find something off the rack, but they can probably get something made-to-measure—with details and finishing made just for them—for roughly 20 percent more in cost.

Why is an unlined suit often more expensive than a lined one?
In an unlined suit, the interior of the jacket is exposed and all the seams are visible. Seams that may normally hide under a lining have to be finished. An unlined suit demonstrates a high level of craftsmanship.

Should I expect alterations to be free, or should I pay for them?
At Nordstrom, all basic alterations on full-price suits are complimentary, from hemming open-bottom pants to taking in the waist, shortening the sleeves on a jacket, and adjusting side or center seams. More complicated alterations require more sewing, and thus more of a tailor's time, so they carry an extra charge.

How many times can I alter a suit based on weight fluctuation?
In terms of the magnitude of weight change, small tweaks are easier to deal with than big ones. If you gain ten pounds, then lose forty, you're better off buying a new suit than yo-yo altering your current one. And if your shoulder measurement changes, alterations won't work. You'll look like you're wearing your dad's jacket.

STYLE TIP:
Never wear a suit more than twice in a week—once a week should be your goal. Varying your look shows more than an investment in your appearance; it demonstrates that you're capable of shifting your mode of thinking and extends the life of your suit.

PUTTING ON A SPORT COAT IS CONSIDERED DE RIGUEUR. INCREDIBLY VERSATILE, THE SPORT COAT IS THE MACGYVER OF CLOTHING—IT CAN UNITE A COMBINATION OF SEEMINGLY RANDOM COMPONENTS INTO SOMETHING THAT MAKES PERFECT SENSE. GENIUS.

THERE'S A REASON THE BLUE BLAZER IS EVERY YOUNG MAN'S INTRODUCTION TO THE WORLD OF TAILORED CLOTHING: IT'S EASY, BASIC, AND SMART. ALTHOUGH SUPERFICIALLY SIMILAR TO THE SUIT JACKET, THE SPORT COAT IS ACTUALLY MUCH MORE VERSATILE.

In recent years, as the world became more casual, the sport coat became a transitional garment. Men attached to suits still had some sense of security pairing a sport coat with khakis. The old rule was that a man should own one sport coat for every four suits, but now it's the reverse. The sport coat is the perfect bridge between the casual world and the formal world.

Sport coats are so versatile, four different guys could wear the same navy blazer, and you wouldn't recognize it. But if you think you're covered just because you have a navy blazer, you're missing out on so many options.

A sport coat is the only piece of clothing you need to travel the world. It's an extra layer in foggy London; perfect with loafers—and no socks—in Miami. In New York, it can take you from the bar at the Four Seasons to the best hot dog stand in town.

NEW NAVY:

The modern sport coat is no longer the traditional blue blazer. It has all the versatility of your favorite hooded sweatshirt—the key is to make it your own. Don't be afraid to experiment; the new generation of menswear designers has retooled the navy blazer with unexpected details including narrower lapels, shorter lengths, and variations on pockets or trim.

ANATOMY OF A SPORT COAT

THE DIFFERENCES BETWEEN THE SUIT JACKET AND THE SPORT COAT ARE SUBTLE BUT SIGNIFICANT. SLIGHT VARIATIONS IN DETAIL GIVE THE SPORT COAT A RELAXED, CASUAL FEELING THAT CONTRASTS WITH A SUIT JACKET'S FORMALITY.

❶ BUTTONS

Most sport coats and blazers have shank buttons. A shank button attaches to the garment via a loop on its backside rather than by two holes in its center. Gold, silver, or bronze buttons are classic on a blazer, but many men shy away from them these days because their look can be less than subtle. Navy plastic buttons are a modern alternative to metallic ones—monochromatic and unobtrusive. On a patterned sport coat, horn or even leather buttons communicate luxury and distinguish the sport coat from a suit jacket.

❷ PATCH POCKETS

Patch pockets provide the main visual distinction between sport coats and suit jackets. They are sewn onto the body of the jacket rather than cut into it, lending a casual look. Not all sport coats and blazers have patch pockets, but most do.

❸ LINING

Like some suit jackets, many blazers and sport coats are unlined, especially when they're meant to be layered on as outerwear.

DID YOU KNOW?
"Sport coat" is a general term that refers to any tailored jacket that's not part of a suit. A blazer is a solid-colored, usually navy wool, sport coat.

SPORT COATS COME IN EVERY FABRIC UNDER THE SUN. FROM WOOL TO LINEN, LEATHER TO SEERSUCKER, A JACKET'S FABRIC COMMUNICATES A SURPRISING AMOUNT ABOUT THE MAN WEARING IT. EVEN SOMEONE WHO KNOWS NOTHING ABOUT MENSWEAR DRAWS CERTAIN CONCLUSIONS ABOUT THAT FELLOW IN TWEED—HE MUST BE SMART—OR THE GUY WHO LOOKS SO COMFORTABLE IN CLASSIC NAVY—HE GREW UP GOING TO A PRIVATE SCHOOL. WHAT DO YOU WANT YOUR JACKET'S FABRIC TO SAY ABOUT YOU?

WOOL
We've already sung wool's virtues for suits. It is the quintessential fabric for blazers, too—especially in navy. Navy is as neutral as black or brown; there's no color it doesn't go with.

VELVET
Velvet gets a bad rap. The word alone may conjure up images of 1970s rock stars and Las Vegas lounge singers, but velvet can be subtle and classic in rich, dark colors.

CORDUROY
Usually made from cotton, corduroy has vertical ribs and a cozy, solid feel. It's probably the most casual fabric for sport coats, and it looks great with jeans.

CASHMERE
Woven from fine goat hair, cashmere has all the benefits of wool, with a cozy bonus: an almost other-worldly softness.

STRIPED   **CHECKED**   **HOUNDSTOOTH**   **GLEN PLAID**

MOST OF THE FIT GUIDELINES FOR SPORT COATS AND BLAZERS ARE THE SAME AS THOSE FOR SUITS. THERE ARE A FEW ADDITIONAL POINTS, THOUGH, THAT HAVE TO DO WITH THE SPORT COAT'S VERSATILITY.

When you're fitting your sport coat, consider the weather in which you'll wear it. Is the coat made of a rugged, cool-weather fabric? Then try it on over a sweater as well as a dress shirt to ensure it will be roomy enough to accommodate under layers. Side vents are also handy if you plan to wear your jacket as an outerwear piece.

If you're shopping for a lightweight summer jacket, try it on with just a T-shirt as well as a dress shirt, to make sure it's not too big.

Also take into account which bottoms you're going to wear the sport coat with. If you'll be wearing it with khakis or jeans, rather than trousers, think about selecting a longer length that allows for more versatility. Shorter jackets go well with casual pants, but such a look can be a bit fashion-forward for some men.

In recent years, the shape of the sport coat has evolved. It's become acceptable to take the "sport" out of "sport coat"; there's no longer a need to portray an enhanced, overly masculine, athletic silhouette. These days, sport coats are deconstructed and comfortable, easy to move around in. They actually feel sporty, instead of just looking that way.

Though the overall fit of a sport coat mirrors that of a suit jacket, there are distinct nuances that distinguish its style.

1 HACKING POCKETS
A British invention, these pockets are diagonally set flap pockets. (Those cheeky Brits are always putting their own stamp on things.)

2 ELBOW PATCHES
The elbows of some blazers and sport coats—especially ones made of heavier fabrics such as tweed or corduroy—are reinforced with patches. Even though we rarely play sports in blazers, these patches help to give a sport coat a relaxed feeling. They're also ideal for arm wrestling champions.

3 LAPELS
Unlike suit jacket lapels, the lapels on a sport coat are sometimes made in a contrasting fabric to the rest of the coat.

4 BUTTONS
Just like suit jackets, sport coats are available with a varying number of buttons. While the jury is out on whether buttons add or subtract height, no man can go wrong with a two- or three-button style.

DID YOU KNOW?
There's some controversy about the origin of the word "blazer." Some say it was born on a British ship—the HMS *Blazer*—in the 1860s. Others say it describes the bright color of jackets worn by a boating club in Cambridge, England.

BLAZERS AND SPORT COATS CAN GET AWAY WITH MANY MORE DETAILS THAN SUIT JACKETS. EACH COAT'S IDIOSYNCRASIES SET IT APART FROM THE REST. HERE ARE THE MOST DISTINCTIVE EXAMPLES.

PIQUÉ STITCHING
These visible stitches convey a sense of craftsmanship and provide a touch of old-fashioned tailoring.

NOVELTY BUTTONS
Whether brass or horn, embossed or not, unusual buttons have been at home on the blazer since its inception.

WORKING BUTTONS
Being able to unfasten the sleeves of a jacket means you can roll up your sleeves—for the sake of fashion or weather.

SHANK BUTTONS
These buttons are sewn onto a jacket through a loop on their backside rather than through two holes in their center.

ELBOW PATCH
Conveying an old-school, professorial vibe, elbow patches used to serve as reinforcements and help a jacket last longer. Now they are decorative.

PEN AND CELL PHONE POCKETS
Find these in your jacket's lining. Be sure to stash your stuff in here and not in your outside pockets!

PATCH POCKETS
Sewn directly onto the front of the jacket instead of set into it, these provide a sporty distinction between a sport coat and suit jacket.

CONTRASTING COLLAR
A jacket made of more than one material has an additional layer of luxury.

THE SPORT COAT IS TRULY THE CLOSET STAPLE FOR THE MODERN MAN–THE ULTIMATE INVESTMENT. NO MATTER WHICH STYLE TYPE YOU ARE, THAT SPORT COAT WILL TAKE YOU FROM THE OFFICE TO DINNER, BECOMING THE MOST VERSATILE PIECE YOU OWN.

LUXURY
Invest in a cardigan.

CLASSIC
Invigorate your casual look.

CONTEMPORARY
Mix fabrics and patterns.

END

a preppy spin on cutting-edge denim.

SPORT COAT FOUR WAYS

THE FOLLOWING LOOKS SHOW HOW DIFFERENT THE SAME JACKET CAN LOOK ON FOUR DISTINCT STYLE TYPES. EACH ONE OF THESE OUTFITS HIGHLIGHTS THE QUINTESSENTIAL BLAZER, WHOSE QUALITY WOOL AND DISTINCT DETAILS GO THE EXTRA MILE FOR YOUR DOLLAR, NO MATTER HOW OR WHERE YOU WEAR IT.

LUXURY

A navy blazer with tailored grey flannel trousers, worn with a vest and classic horse-bit loafers, is masculine and polished.

CLASSIC

This is Casual Friday redux with polished, high-quality pieces and no tie. You can't go wrong with an argyle sweater.

CONTEMPORARY

A blazer with jeans is
the ultimate in urbane.
A fancy shirt and stylish
shoes make things
look pulled together
yet effortless.

TREND

With the right layers,
a blazer can act as
the ultimate piece
of outerwear. The
cardigan and canvas
shoes add a rock 'n'
roll touch.

FALL SPORT COATS

WEARING A BLAZER IN FALL IS THE PERFECT WAY TO EXPERIMENT WITH RICH, WARM TEXTURES. ALL FOUR OF THESE LOOKS EXPRESS STRONG, MASCULINE STYLE IN THEIR OWN WAY—WHICH IS QUINTESSENTIALLY NORDSTROM.

LUXURY

Sometimes you can get the dressiness of a sport coat with the coziness of a sweater. British touches provide a jaunty style.

CLASSIC

Here's an updated spin on a country gentleman look: a tweed jacket with soft shoulders, suede elbow patches, and open patch pockets.

TREND

Three classic pieces
combined in an unexpected
way—a dark sport coat
worn with a tailored vest
and a hoodie—create the
ultimate hip look for
running around the city.

CONTEMPORARY

Country meets city with a
tailored jacket paired with
classic chinos. A creamy
knit sweater neutralizes
the palette.

TO MIX OR TO MATCH?

PATTERN COMBINING IS AN ELUSIVE SCIENCE–OR ART–DEPENDING ON HOW YOU LOOK AT IT. WHILE THERE'S NO SCIENTIFIC METHOD FOR DETERMINING THE PERFECT JACKET, SHIRT, AND TIE COMBINATIONS, THE FOLLOWING ARE A FEW GUIDELINES THAT WON'T STEER YOU WRONG.

TWO PATTERNS **THREE PATTERNS** **FOUR PATTERNS** **MONOCHROMATIC**

If you're going to wear different patterns together, vary their sizes. If you have a shirt with a fine pattern, you can go for a bolder-patterned tie. If your shirt is bold, go for a finer-patterned tie. It's your basic yin and yang.

Monochromatic always works. Wearing a variety of shades from the same palette looks confident and expensive–think Regis Philbin on pretty much every show he's ever hosted.

Make sure everything you're wearing belongs in the same season. A cashmere sweater looks smart under a wool sport coat; a cotton oxford does well under a khaki blazer. But a thick wool sweater under a linen blazer just looks odd.

ASK THE NORDSTROM TAILOR

I've recently lost some weight, and my blazer feels a bit loose. How difficult would it be to take in?

The rules for fitting a blazer are the same as those for fitting a suit jacket—shoulders are key. If you've been working out a lot—keeping the bulk of your shoulders intact but slimming down around the waist—the alterations should be no problem. If, however, you're an actor preparing for a role as an athlete, or you've been surviving on protein shakes, you may need to buy a new jacket.

I've put on a few pounds, and the buttons on my sport coat are pulling. How far can they be moved over?

It's not so much a matter of moving buttons but of letting out the sport coat's side seams, which have about an inch of extra fabric to work with on each side. You can also move the buttons slightly, but too much movement can throw the coat off-balance. Your tailor will know which method to use in order to give you a little extra room.

What are the rules for buttoning a jacket?

No matter how many buttons you elect to have on your jacket, you should always leave at least one of them unbuttoned—preferably the bottom one—unless you want to look like your mother dressed you.

Can you turn a blazer into a dinner jacket or vest?

Short answer: No! Some might say you can contemporize a blazer by adding tape trim to the lapels or fancying up the buttons. We say leave the fashion design to *Project Runway*.

STYLE TIP:
Keep a blazer in your office for unforeseen circumstances. The ideal specs? Midnight blue, performance wool, single-breasted, natural shoulder. This will dress up anything you're wearing and make you feel stylish in virtually any situation.

TROUS

PANTS ARE THE ONE CLOTHING ITEM A MAN PUTS ON VIRTUALLY
EVERY SINGLE DAY OF HIS LIFE. TROUSERS ARE SPECIAL, HOWEVER.
THE WORD "TROUSERS" REFERS TO A TAILORED GARMENT WITH
DETAILS SUCH AS BELT LOOPS, A FLY, A WAISTBAND, PLEATS,
OR CUFFS. THEY'RE NOT YOUR JEANS OR KHAKIS, BUT PRETTY
MUCH EVERYTHING ELSE. WE'LL CONCERN OURSELVES WITH
TROUSERS IN THIS BOOK, BUT MANY OF THE LESSONS YOU LEARN
HERE CAN BE APPLIED TO YOUR CASUAL PANTS AS WELL.

ANATOMY OF TROUSERS

FLAT-FRONT TROUSERS HAVE EVOLVED, WITH A SILHOUETTE SHIFT AND NEW CONSTRUCTION TECHNIQUES. THE ONCE-FORMAL TROUSER HAS MORPHED INTO A SIMPLE, COMFORTABLE PAIR OF PANTS YOU'LL WANT TO WEAR AS MUCH AS YOUR FAVORITE KHAKIS.

1 SIDE TABS

More common on trousers than suit pants, side tabs allow the wearer of a pair of pants to play with the garment's waist circumference. They can have a bit of a vintage look, and they are most helpful to the guy whose waist is a bit small in proportion to his hips and backside.

2 RISE

The rise refers to the length of the zipper, from the crotch to the waistband. The rise on a pair of suit trousers should fit as high and close as is comfortable, since this will actually make moving around easier and decrease the stress on the fabric. Thus, properly fitted pants will last longer than ill-fitting ones.

3 INSEAM

The inseam is the length of the pant leg from the crotch to the hem. Depending on the style of pants and the finishing you choose, this measurement can vary a little.

4 BREAK

When someone's pants are too short, you may think, *Hey, that guy should have a party and invite his pants to meet his shoes.* The break is that party.

A **full break** covers almost the whole top of the shoe and leaves a deep horizontal crease at the front of the pant leg.

A **medium break** is the most popular option and stops at the highest point of the instep.

A **short break** covers just the top quarter inch of the shoe and can produce a bit of a growth-spurt effect, so it's only for the fashion-forward.

5 HEM

Cuffed trousers are the same length all around; since they're wider, they hang straight.

Cuffless trousers are hemmed so the back falls slightly lower than the front.

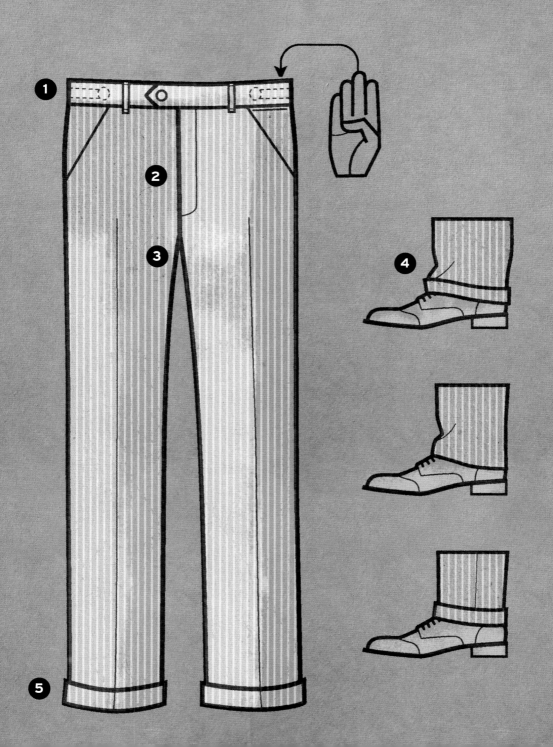

fabric

DID YOU KNOW?
There are two pairs of trousers every man should have: grey wool and khaki cotton.

YOU'VE ALREADY SEEN THE MOST COMMON TROUSER FABRICS IN THE SUITS CHAPTER, SO WE WON'T REPEAT THEM HERE. BELOW ARE THE ESSENTIAL FABRICS FOR TROUSERS THAT FLY SOLO. THESE ARE THE ONES THAT YOU'LL WEAR WITH A BLAZER, SPORT COAT, OR SWEATER RATHER THAN WITH A SUIT JACKET.

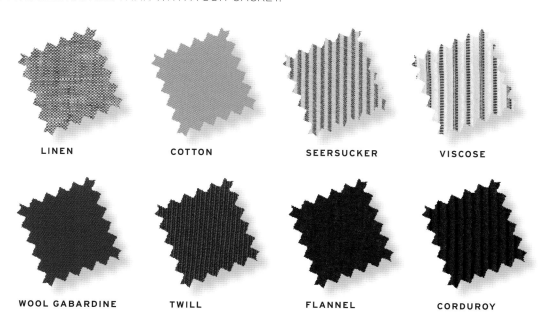

LINEN　　**COTTON**　　**SEERSUCKER**　　**VISCOSE**

WOOL GABARDINE　　**TWILL**　　**FLANNEL**　　**CORDUROY**

THE WAY WE FIT TROUSERS HAS CHANGED MARKEDLY IN THE PAST DECADE. FOR MUCH OF THE TWENTIETH CENTURY, AMERICAN MEN WORE PLEATED TROUSERS THAT FASTENED AT THE HIGH POINT OF THE WAIST, DRAPING LOOSELY OVER THE STOMACH AND CASCADING TO THE FLOOR IN WIDE, OFTEN CUFFED, LEGS. IN RECENT YEARS, THE MOST POPULAR SILHOUETTE HAS BECOME A BIT SLEEKER, SITTING JUST SLIGHTLY LOWER ON THE TORSO, WITH A SLIMMER LEG AND, OFTEN, NO PLEATS OR CUFFS.

Regardless of which type of pants you choose, the key fit points are the same:

❶ WAIST

A surprising number of men have no idea where their natural waist is. It's the spot *above* your hip bones but below your navel, the part of your torso with the smallest circumference. This is the place to measure in order to determine your pant size. Some of you may find the idea of wearing your trousers at your waist (and not hanging from your hips) a little square. Consider that when a waistband hits just above your hips and not under them, the hips can support the pants, which means your stomach no longer needs to be strangled by a tourniquet masquerading as a belt. Don't be afraid to let the waist out a bit or even buy the next size up—no one's looking at the *inside* of your waistband.

TRADITIONAL

The traditional waistband is constructed in its entirety before it's sewn onto the body of the pants. A piece of canvas hidden inside the outer and inner fabrics helps it hold its shape.

CONTINENTAL

Sometimes called an extended-tab waistband, the continental has a piece of fabric that extends toward the right hip, as well as one external and one internal button that prevent gaping.

HOLLYWOOD

The Hollywood waistband is made from the pants themselves, not sewn on separately. It sits high on the waist, sometimes with Rat Pack-style dropped belt loops and a center back notch.

❷ LEG SHAPE

It's best to avoid exaggerated leg shapes. The width of a pant's leg should be dictated by its waist, with the fabric draping all the way down to the break and tapering ever so slightly. It follows naturally, then, that plain-front trousers usually have a pretty straight leg, while pleated ones start out a little fuller at the hip. The bottom leg opening of a pair of pants should balance the size of your shoes.

❸ SLASH POCKETS

Cut on an angle, slash pockets can pull open if pants are snug.

DID YOU KNOW?
Your pants are too small when the pleats strain across the front or your pockets pull open.

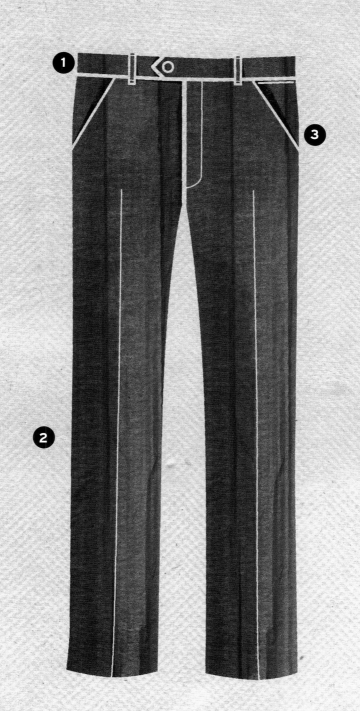

PANTS ARE DESIGNED WITH PRECISE DETAILS THAT ARE INHERENT TO THE VERY FUNCTION OF THE GARMENT AND THE COMFORT OF THE WEARER—REGARDLESS OF YOUR STYLE TYPE OR BODY SHAPE.

BUTTON FLY
Old-fashioned and often considered a sign of high quality, a button fly diminishes fears of snagging and catching. It's also easier to mend than a zipper.

DOUBLE-BUTTON CLOSURE
This extended tab closure gives the waist extra stability and staying power.

ZIP FLY
Quick and easy, the zip fly gives a smooth appearance. Just be sure the zipper isn't too long for your rise measurement, or your pants will look sloppy.

SMALL BELT LOOP
To really keep the belt in place, slide part of the buckle through this tiny loop. No more buckle in the back!

WAIST LINING
This slip-proof, breathable fabric liner keeps pants comfortably in place.

BESOM POCKET
Common on single-pleat pants, the besom pocket is finished with a clean, simple edge.

PATCH POCKET
One or two of these positioned on the backside of a pair of pants gives a casual feeling—and a good place to stash your wallet.

CUFFS
Just like any optional detail, cuffs go in and out of fashion. While right now we're in the midst of a low-cuff cycle, things could change with the drop of a hat. So concern yourself not with what's in or out but with what looks good on you.

LUXURY
Flat-front trousers
create a slim look.

CLASSIC
Single-pleat trousers have
a loose, forgiving fit.

TREND
Extra-slim pants with an
extended tab are trendy
and body-conscious.

CONTEMPORARY
Pinstripes can be elongating.

NORDSTROM IS KNOWN FOR ITS INCREDIBLE SELECTION OF SHOES. THERE'S NO WAY WE COULD ADEQUATELY ADDRESS THE BREADTH AND VARIETY OF OPTIONS AVAILABLE IN FOOTWEAR HERE. NO MATTER WHAT YOUR STYLE TYPE, EVERY MAN CAN BENEFIT FROM A STANDOUT COLLECTION OF SHOES. I ENCOURAGE YOU TO APPROACH YOUR SHOE WARDROBE WITH THE SAME ENTHUSIASM YOU BRING TO SELECTING YOUR TAILORED CLOTHING. AFTER ALL, YOUR SHOES ALLOW YOU TO PUT YOUR BEST FOOT FORWARD.

A FEW OF MY FAVORITE TIPS:

- A suit is a more formal expression; consequently your footwear should complement that look. Oxfords (lace-ups) are the most appropriate choice.

- A sport coat, or more casual slacks and a collared shirt, look best with a loafer, driver, or less formal oxford.

- Shoes in brown (or a shade of brown) are appropriate for most suits and sport coats, including navy and lighter shades of grey. Black shoes are preferred for black, darker greys, and navy suits, when you want a more conservative look.

- Avoid heavy, dark shoes during the summer. In warm weather, you always want to look as comfortable as you feel.

WHAT TO WEAR WITH ...

Wool/flannel: Wing-tip or cap-toe oxfords in brown suede.
Linen: Steer toward earth-toned or tan-colored shoes or loafers, with or without socks.
Seersucker/cotton: White or neutral-colored bucks.
Denim: Lug soles, loafers, and sneakers offer you urban-to-suburban style.

When my tailor asks whether I want cuffs, I have no idea. What am I supposed to say?
Flat-front pants look best without a cuff; pleated pants look best with one. Why? Draping. Pleated pants have extra fabric, and a cuff anchors it with a bit of weight so it can flow easily over the leg.
If you want to make your legs look longer, just say no to cuffs. They cut legs off at the ankle, which, of course, can make them appear shorter.

Should there be a difference in length between my summer pants and my winter ones?
That depends entirely on your shoes. If you plan to wear flip-flops or other similarly low-soled shoes with your trousers in the summertime, wear them to the tailor's in order to ensure the hems of your pants won't drag under your exposed heels.

Can a tailor convert a pair of pleated pants into flat-front ones?
While this alteration is technically possible, it is complex. Flat-front pants often have a shorter rise than pleated ones, which means you won't only be removing pleats but also shortening the crotch. Since pleated pants have a fuller cut, their front and back will be different widths. In addition, the pockets may need to be adjusted or replaced. The leg shape will also be affected. While a master tailor will try to deliver a balanced, well-fitting trouser, you're much better off looking for a new pair of pants.

Is it true that pleats look dated?
Though fashion-conscious guys sometimes give pleats a bad rap, they've been a staple of men's tailoring for years and they're not going anywhere. Well-placed pleats can camouflage extra weight and balance a man's proportions. They work well for broad and athletic body types. One pleat—rather than two—is enough for most men, lending a bit of camouflage and some leg width. Two pleats make a statement. Unless you're careful that they fit impeccably and are executed in a gorgeous fabric, that statement might be, "Welcome to 1991!"

DID YOU KNOW?
The first pockets were pouches that hung from a belt.

AS THE SAYING GOES, IF YOU REALLY CARE ABOUT SOMEONE, YOU ARE WILLING TO GIVE THEM THE SHIRT OFF YOUR BACK. IT FOLLOWS, THEN, THAT SHIRTS MUST BE PRETTY IMPORTANT. THE SHIRT IS THE PART OF THE TAILORED ENSEMBLE THAT SITS CLOSEST TO THE BODY, SO IT HAS TO BE COMFORTABLE AND IMPECCABLY FITTED. EVEN THOUGH IT MAY SEEM ALMOST INVISIBLE, A GREAT SHIRT IS WHAT MAKES A GREAT SUIT LOOK, WELL, GREAT. THE SHIRT IS THE HEART OF THE SUIT—THE JELLY IN THE DOUGHNUT, THE OLIVE IN THE MARTINI. READ ON TO FIND THE CENTER OF YOUR SARTORIAL UNIVERSE.

ANATOMY OF A SHIRT

1 COLLAR

2 PLACKET

3 YOKE

4 POCKET

5 BUTTONS

6 SLEEVE

7 CUFF

DID YOU KNOW?
Most shirts used to have detachable cuffs and collars. This meant much less laundry before the days of washing machines. Jealous?

MANY MEN KEEP THEIR RELATIONSHIPS WITH THEIR FAVORITE FABRIC CLOSE TO THEIR CHESTS, LITERALLY. WE IDENTIFY WHAT WE LIKE AS TEENAGERS AND RARELY STRAY FROM OUR PREFERENCES LATER IN LIFE.

Whatever kind of fabric you favor, chances are it's cotton. Natural fibers are even more important in a shirt than in a jacket. Why? Because a shirt sits closest to your skin. Durability, crispness, comfort—nearly all the elements of a great shirt are due to the fabric from which it's made. Cotton is comfortable and breathable, absorbent and static-resistant.

Cotton quality is determined largely by the length of its fibers. American pima and Egyptian cotton—whether grown in the United States, in Egypt, or even in the West Indies—have extra-long fibers that result in finer, smoother, and softer fabric than cloth made from cottons with short fibers.

There are many kinds of cotton weaves, from oxford to pinpoint, twill to herringbone. (See the swatches to your right.) An oxford shirt is the ultimate classic—it can be worn in so many different ways. When it's laundered and starched, it is substantial and serious—the perfect shirt for business. Machine-washed and softened, it becomes as comfortable as a pajama top, but infinitely hipper. A second skin with maximum versatility. Depending on how you care for an oxford, it takes on its own form—much like jeans, it's shrink-to-fit.

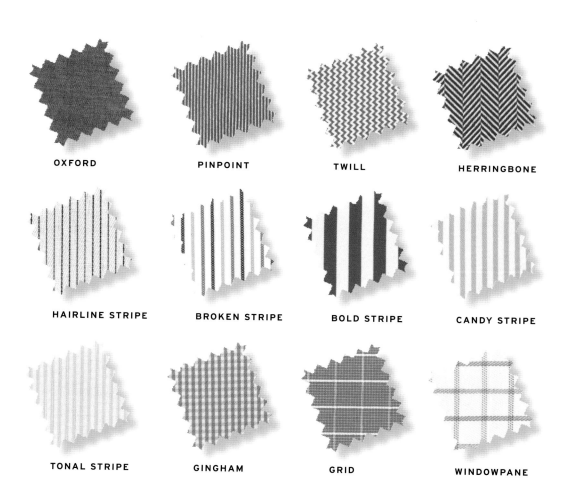

OXFORD   PINPOINT   TWILL   HERRINGBONE

HAIRLINE STRIPE   BROKEN STRIPE   BOLD STRIPE   CANDY STRIPE

TONAL STRIPE   GINGHAM   GRID   WINDOWPANE

DID YOU KNOW?

Organics: They're not just for the salad bar anymore. Organic cotton is defined by the same principles as those for any other organic crop—no pesticides, responsible farming practices—and besides being better for the environment, it produces a finer cloth as well.

THE FIT OF A SHIRT REFERS TO THE MEASUREMENTS OF ITS NECK, CHEST, WAIST, AND BOTTOM OPENING. WE'LL TALK ABOUT DETAILS SUCH AS COLLARS, CUFFS, AND PLACKETS IN THE NEXT SECTION. YOUR SHIRT SIZE IS DESCRIBED IN TERMS OF TWO MEASUREMENTS: YOUR NECK CIRCUMFERENCE AND YOUR SLEEVE LENGTH. OF COURSE, THE NUMBERS DON'T ACTUALLY EQUAL YOUR NECK CIRCUMFERENCE OR YOUR SLEEVE LENGTH—ARE THINGS EVER THAT SIMPLE? HERE'S HOW TO DETERMINE THEM:

1 NECK WIDTH

Starting at your Adam's apple, wrap a measuring tape around your neck. Note the actual measurement, then add 1 inch to determine your size. The number should be somewhere between 14 and 19 inches.

When a shirt's neck hole measurement is right, its collar won't droop—it will form a perfect V shape along with your tie without revealing even a glimpse of your windpipe. If you feel the need to tighten your tie frequently, you know your shirt is too big. On the other hand, you should always be able to comfortably fit two fingers between your neck and your collar.

2 SLEEVE LENGTH

Measure from the nape of your neck to the bottom of your wrist. Remember that your shirtsleeve should extend ½ inch beyond your jacket sleeve.

If all this measuring sounds like a nightmare, don't worry—every Nordstrom salesperson can do it for you.

Once you know your shirt size, it's time to pick a silhouette based on your body type and style. Most shirts come in one of three silhouettes: classic, tailored, and trim.

3 CLASSIC SHIRT

Cut full through the chest, waist, and arm holes.

Best for: Broad, Athletic

4 TAILORED SHIRT

More body-conscious than a classic fit, this streamlined style fits a little closer to the chest, and a lot closer to the waist.

Best for: Lanky, Compact, Athletic

5 TRIM SHIRT

Slim all over, this silhouette is for the guy who wants absolutely no extra fabric to bunch under his jacket.

Best for: Lanky, Compact

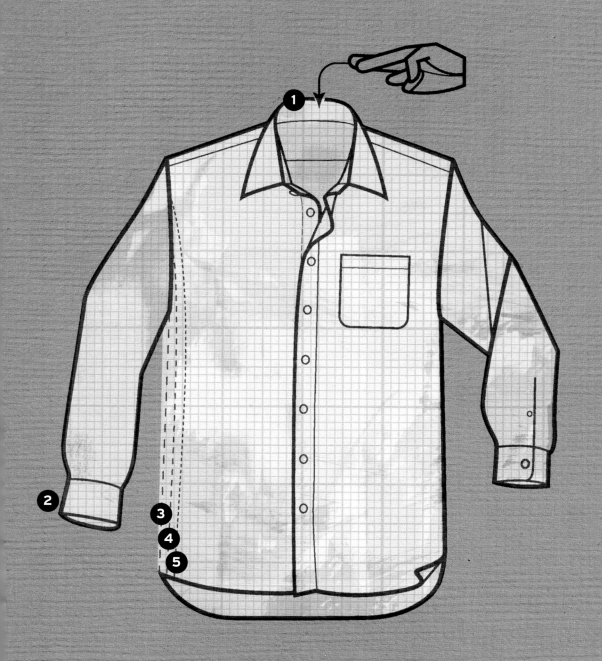

NO ONE PART OF A SHIRT SHOULD OUTSHINE THE OTHERS. COLLARS, CUFFS, PLACKETS, AND BUTTONS CAN BE SUBLIME IN THEIR SIMPLICITY. YOU ONLY NEED TO REMEMBER ONE THING WHEN IT COMES TO PROPORTION AND DETAILS: BALANCE.

POINT COLLAR
You can't go wrong with the point collar—it's the most versatile collar and is always appropriate for business. Its elongating, double-V shapes look good on every man.

Best for: All style types

SPREAD COLLAR
A step dressier than the point collar, the spread collar looks great with double-breasted suits and flatters men with slim necks. Sometimes referred to as a cutaway, it originated to accommodate the Windsor knot.

Best for: Luxury, Contemporary

BUTTON-DOWN COLLAR
A button-down collar is a point collar secured by two small buttons. You'll never have to think about this one—the buttons should always be buttoned and the collar will stay in place. It's like a plant that doesn't need watering.

Best for: All style types

FRENCH FRONT
This placket is folded under, without a seam, and requires special finishing. It has a formal appearance because the stitching detail is invisible.

Best for: Luxury, Contemporary

RENCH CUFF
haracterized by two
oles lined up next to
ach another, French
uffs lack a built-in
utton. This enables you
o accessorize with the
uff links of your choice
nd gives the impression
our clothes have been
ailored for you.

est for: Luxury,
ontemporary, Trend

BARREL CUFF
Also called a single cuff,
the barrel cuff fastens
with a button and
buttonhole. The most
traditional American
cuff style, it usually
accompanies a classic
point-collar shirt.

CROSS STITCH
Cross-stitching—an X shape
anchoring the button to the
placket—is a must.

STACKED BUTTONS
The thicker the
buttons, like above
right, the higher
quality and more
durable they are.

THE WHITE SHIRT IS A MAN'S WARDROBE STAPLE. IT SEEMS SIMPLE, BUT AS WE'VE ALREADY LEARNED, THE MAGIC IS IN THE DETAILS. YOU'D BE SURPRISED AT HOW MANY PLACES THE RIGHT WHITE SHIRT CAN TAKE YOU, FROM A FORMAL AFFAIR TO THE OFFICE TO A WEEKEND BRUNCH, LAYERED OVER A T-SHIRT. A WHITE SHIRT'S CLEAN LINES AND APPEARANCE ARE SO ADDICTIVE, YOU'LL WANT ONE FOR EVERY DAY OF THE WEEK.

LUXURY   CLASSIC   CONTEMPORARY

END

ASK THE NORDSTROM TAILOR

Why would I buy a made-to-measure shirt instead of an off-the-rack one?
Commissioning a made-to-order shirt allows you to choose exactly the details you want, from cuff style and buttons to fabric and pattern. Basically, you get to play designer without worrying about messing things up. Made-to-measure shirts are ideal for men whose measurements are unusual—a neck circumference or arm length that is larger or smaller than average.

I'm retiring. What will I do with all my dress shirts?
So many men donate their shirts once they stop wearing suits every day. But you can continue to wear your shirts well beyond your office days if you know how to care for and style them casually. First, transition from professionally cleaning your shirts to washing them at home. This will remove any stiff starchiness, and give them a more relaxed look. When putting an outfit together, layer an untucked shirt over a T-shirt. Toss that tie, roll up your sleeves, and unbutton your top button to communicate ease and sophistication.

Do people still monogram their shirts?
Monogramming is a great way to make a shirt your own—and make sure the dry cleaner doesn't confuse it with someone else's. When opting to monogram, remember this simple rule: one shirt, one monogram—cuff, pocket, or waist. The cuff is the most popular place to put a monogram. Be careful when branding patterned shirts—choose a font and color that blend in. You want to complement but not overpower your shirt.

How do I know if I'm getting a good-quality shirt?
First, feel the fabric. Like nice sheets, it should be smooth but sturdy, with a uniform weave, and not see-through. Next, check out the buttons. They should be made from a natural material such as mother-of-pearl (opalescent and much stronger than plastic), and be stacked (picture poker chips atop one another). They should be cross-stitched tightly to the placket. For patterns, make sure they line up at the seams.

I carry a lot of weight in the middle, and I notice shirts seem to be getting slimmer. Will I be able to find anything to wear?
Shirts are getting slimmer in order to accommodate trimmer suit silhouettes. Substantial guys can still find something to wear, though—just look for a style with box pleats, which allow for more body in the shirt.

What does "wrinkle-free" mean?
A wrinkle-free shirt is treated with a coating that prevents wrinkling during wear and reduces ironing time. Nordstrom offers Smartcare, a proprietary coating applied to select 100-percent-cotton Nordstrom shirts.

What are collar stays?
Collar stays are small, thin tabs, pointed at one end and rounded at the other, that slip into the points of a shirt collar in order to make them lie flat. They come in a variety of materials, from metal to plastic to mother-of-pearl. Remove them before laundering or dry cleaning.

NECKW

WHERE DID THE IDEA FOR THE NECKTIE COME FROM, ANYWAY? WHO THOUGHT, LET'S TAKE A DECORATIVE PIECE OF SHINY CLOTH–FESTOONED WITH PAISLEYS, CHECKS, STRIPES, DOTS, WHATEVER STRIKES YOUR FANCY–AND WRAP IT AROUND THE NECK TO COMMUNICATE CONFIDENCE AND MASCULINITY? SEVENTEENTH-CENTURY CROATIANS DID, AND THEN THE REST OF THE WORLD FOLLOWED SUIT.

THE NECKTIE HAS ALWAYS SPOKEN MULTITUDES ABOUT OUR CULTURE. IT WAS SKINNY AND MODERN IN THE '60S, FUN AND EXAGGERATED IN THE '70S, AND RICH AND THICK IN THE '80S. THEN, FOR A WHILE, IT SEEMED TO DISAPPEAR ALTOGETHER. NOW THIS ICONIC PIECE OF FABRIC IS BACK AND BETTER THAN EVER.

Whether you want to appear subtle and dignified, or to distinguish yourself as a trendsetter, the necktie is a bold and economical way to make a statement. With more widths and fabrics available than ever before, you never need an excuse to spend some time in the neckwear department. Just don't blame me when the addiction kicks in—this is one vice I'm happy to endorse.

ANATOMY OF A TIE

THERE'S MORE TO A TIE THAN MEETS THE EYE.

1 INNER LINING

Helps the tie hold its shape and gives it weight so that it will hang properly. The highest-quality linings are 100 percent wool. Self-tipping is when a tie is lined with the same fabric as its body.

2 KEEPER LOOP

The loop label is where a manufacturer does its branding, but the keeper loop also serves a purpose: It allows the tail of the necktie to lie flat. It's amazing how many guys who've been wearing ties for years fail to realize they can tuck the back of their tie into the loop label to ensure it lies flat.

3 SLIP STITCH

A loose black thread found woven through the back of the tie, the slip stitch keeps the tie from losing its shape through lots of knotting.

4 BAR TACK STITCH

The bar tack stitch connects the two back flaps and keeps them lying flat.

5 DIMPLE

A subtle but crucial signifier of style, it's up to you to create the dimple when you tie your knot.

6 TIE LENGTH

A tie should be long enough to reach the waistband of your trousers after it's tied. The tip of the tie should hit the belt buckle.

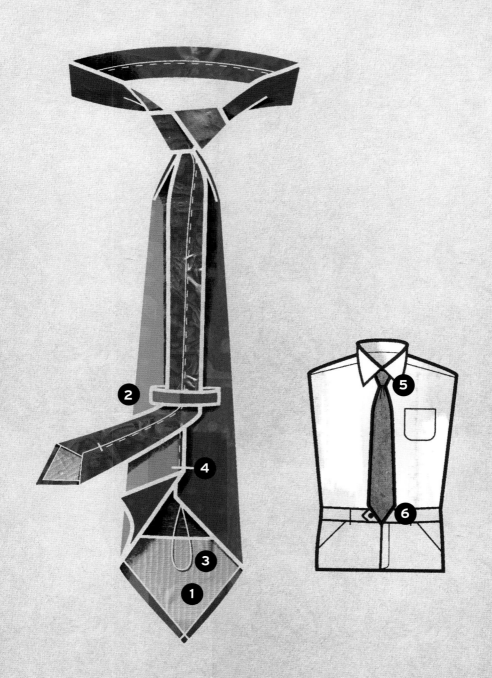

fabric

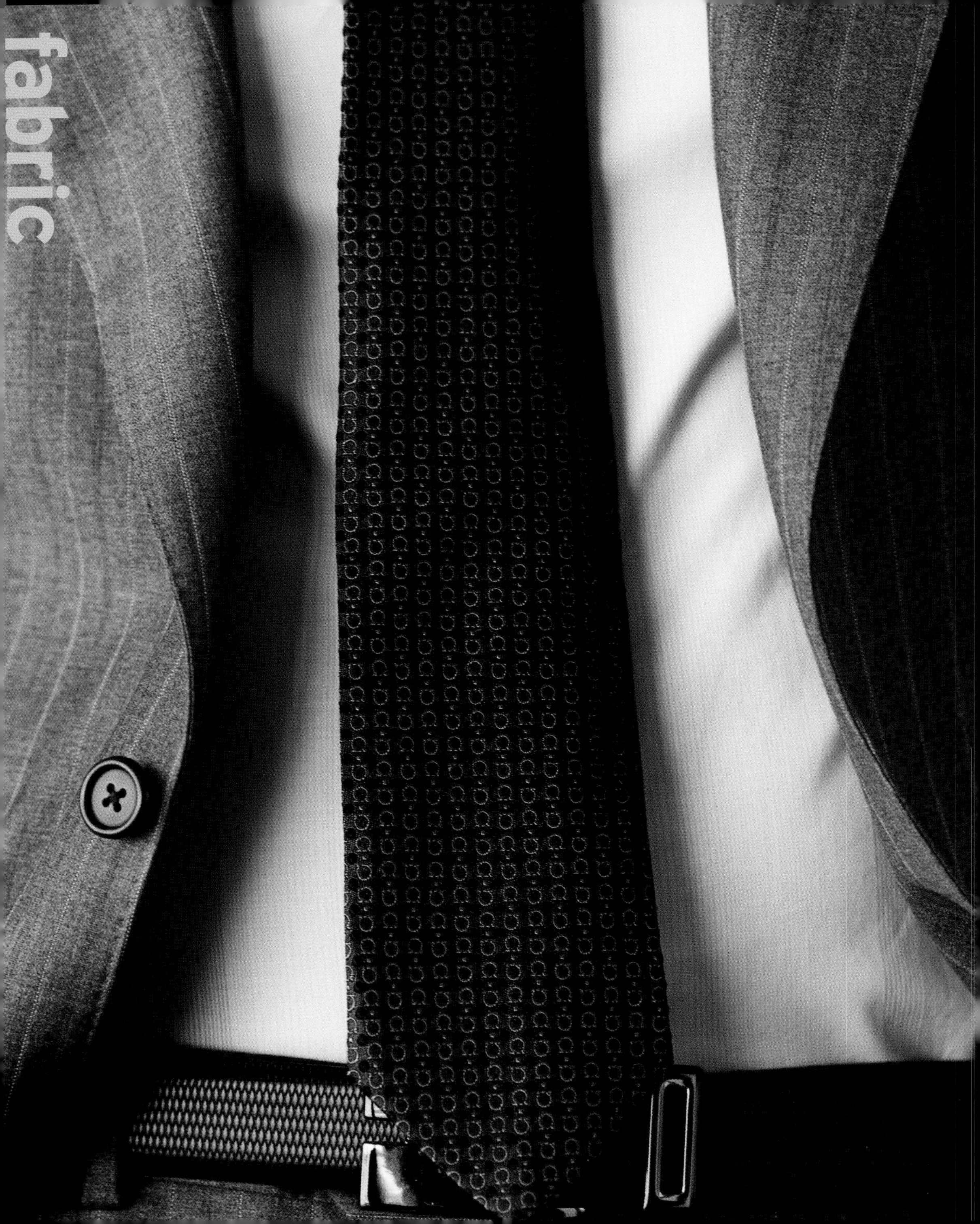

TIES ARE AVAILABLE IN LITERALLY MILLIONS OF FABRICS AND PATTERNS.
HERE ARE SOME OF THE MOST COMMON ONES.

REPP STRIPE

SOLID

POLKA DOT

NEAT/FOULARD

PLAID

PAISLEY

STYLE TIP:
Choose the highest-quality tie you can. The fabric should be smooth,
not rough. Always pass up a tie with sewing mistakes or puckers.

FOUR-IN-HAND

The most common tie knot, the four-in-hand can be worn with any collar style. No matter what, you'll get a clean and simple knot and you can vary its length according to what suits your body. The four-in-hand projects quiet confidence without drawing attention to the neck or throwing the proportion of the jacket off-balance.

Best for: All style types

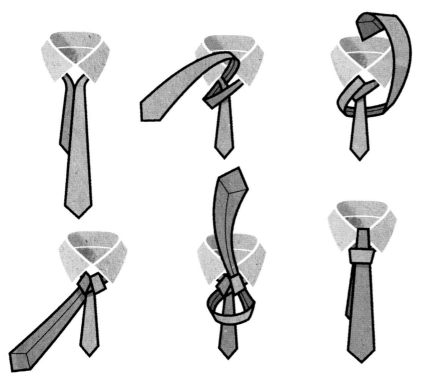

WINDSOR

The biggest and bulkiest knot, the Windsor is at home paired with a spread collar. This knot belongs to the world of finance and power lunches—it's immaculately finished in every way.

Best for: Luxury, Classic

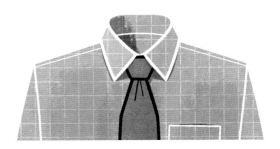

HALF-WINDSOR

A step more formal than the four-in-hand, the half-Windsor knot is substantial, distinguished, and traditional—perfect for special occasions.

Best for: All style types

BOW TIE

With a fun, nostalgic quality, the bow tie is quintessentially American. While we offer a diagram at left for tying the bow tie, don't attempt it unless you're a connoisseur. Go for the pre-tied wraparound version—we promise not to tell!

Best for: Luxury, Classic

DO YOU REALIZE HOW MANY CHOICES ARE AVAILABLE WHEN IT COMES TO NECKWEAR, BEYOND THE OBVIOUS TIE?

CRAVAT

Simply put, the cravat is neckwear wrapped around the neck but not knotted. Like the ascot, it can be a lot to pull off—but also packs a payoff.

BOW TIE

Classically American, the bow tie is still considered a traditional style—but in the right color and pattern can be fun.

Fit note: If your neck is thicker, don't choose a bow tie. Instead, draw attention downward with a traditional necktie.

ASCOT

With a touch of irony and a ton of style, this wink to high society is back in fashion. A double-knotted tie with one end draped over the other, or knotted for a more casual look, the ascot is named after an English racetrack where it was worn.

NECKTIE

Tie width is a barometer of where fashion is going. A medium-width tie is always safe, where extra-narrow and extra-wide ones often scream, "fashion statement!" Try to choose your tie width so it's in proportion with the lapels of your jacket.

SEVEN-FOLD TIE
Made of just one piece of fabric folded seven times by expert craftsmen, the seven-fold tie feels thicker and more substantial than mass-produced ties. Wearing one is like a secret handshake: Insiders will recognize its quality.

SCARF
Scarves have evolved from being an outerwear piece to being an accessory. In silk, cotton, or wool, scarves look great with suits, sport coats, or even without a jacket. Stay away from heavyweight wools and puffy yarns; instead, opt for a lightweight linen, wool, or cotton scarf.

BRACES
Also known as suspenders, these are two straps worn over the shoulders that cross in back. Braces allow pants to hang properly because you're not constricting your waistband with a belt.

Note: Braces fasten with buttons and suspenders fasten with clips.

POCKET SQUARE
Although this small piece of fabric evolved from the handkerchief, it was always meant to be decorative rather than useful. A pocket square lends distinction, luxury, and modernity.

Note: Your pocket square should not match your tie.

TIES ARE ALL ABOUT PATTERN, TEXTURE, AND DIMENSION—ALL IN ONE PLACE. PUTTING TOGETHER A SHIRT AND TIE IS AN EXCELLENT WAY TO EXPRESS YOUR STYLE TYPE. HERE ARE SOME IDEAS FOR INSPIRATION:

LUXURY

It takes a confident guy to pair a striped shirt with a patterned tie. These combos work for two reasons: Both pieces are in the same color palette, and the patterns are scaled differently from the shirts.

CLASSIC

A broadcloth shirt has some color variation, so this combination is more about texture than color or pattern. A tie with a bit of texture or shine will play off a textured shirt. When in doubt about how to mix colors, don't. Stay with monochromatic color choices.

CONTEMPORARY
Pair bold and graphic to be current but not flashy. The white contrast-collar shirt, appropriately accessorized, works well with trousers–sans jacket.

TREND
This is all about pairing stripes and checks in an unexpected way. Adding a narrow tie completes the look.

ASK THE NORDSTROM TAILOR

Mixing shirt and tie patterns is a challenge. Is there a simple rule?
Think of it this way: One should always win—either a bold tie or a bold shirt. When in doubt, let your tie take center stage.

I'm not a fashion guy. How wide should my tie be?
Over the past fifty years, the tie has served as a barometer of fashion. From the skinny, mod '60s to the pumped-up '80s, tie width has been a reflection of society. Your tie will fly below the radar if it measures between 2½ and 3½ inches.

What's the best way to store my ties?
While hanging a tie on cedar tie hangers works, the best way to keep a tie looking great is to store it rolled rather than folded.

DID YOU KNOW?
A tie lies flat because it's cut on the bias—diagonally off the fabric. Because of this construction, even when it's tied, a well-made tie hangs straight down. And, a tie will last longer if untied properly. Instead of slipping the knot out, which stresses the fabric, untie the tie the same way you tied it, but in reverse.

I FIRST STOOD ON THE RED CARPET AS A FASHION COMMENTATOR AT THE ACADEMY AWARDS IN 1995. THIS WAS BEFORE CELEBRITIES WORE INTERNATIONAL DESIGNERS OR ONE-OF-A-KIND PIECES, AND IT WAS A SEA OF SAMENESS. OVER THE YEARS, I WITNESSED THE MEN OF HOLLYWOOD TRANSFORM THE BLACK-TIE LOOK TO MAKE IT THEIR OWN. AND THROUGH THIS EVOLUTION OF PERSONAL STYLE, THE TUX STILL REIGNS SUPREME.

MEN TODAY ARE CHOOSING CLASSIC STYLING WITH AN INTERNATIONAL TWIST, REFLECTING THE INCREASINGLY GLOBAL NATURE OF THE OSCARS AND OF OUR WORLD ITSELF. LOTS OF HIGH-PROFILE GUYS MAKE THEIR TUXES THEIR OWN WITH SIGNATURE TOUCHES—THINK JAMIE FOXX'S CHOICE OF MIDNIGHT BLUE INSTEAD OF BLACK, OR THE SATIN EDGING ON GEORGE CLOONEY'S LAPEL.

TUXEDOS AREN'T SEEN AS PENGUIN SUITS ANYMORE. MANY ARE MADE FROM PERFORMANCE WOOL, SO THEY WILL BREATHE AND MAINTAIN THEIR SHAPE THROUGHOUT A LONG EVENING. THE SHAPE OF THE MODERN TUXEDO REFLECTS THE SHAPE OF THE SUIT, SO REST ASSURED, IF YOU CAN FIND A SUIT YOU LIKE, YOU'LL BE ABLE TO FIND A TUX, TOO.

That said, there are subtle but important fit differences between a suit and a tuxedo. Tuxedo pants are slimmer and higher-waisted than suit pants, and they are never cuffed—ever. And be sure to stay away from anything made of synthetic fibers, such as polyester, because it can encourage perspiration.

A tuxedo's signature decorative details range from stripes and braids on trousers to satin on lapels. Satin is the most traditional choice for accent fabric. It has a subtle sheen and suits all style types. Grosgrain is similar to satin in its shininess, but it has a ribbed texture rather than a flat one, making it a good choice for men who want to stand out.

DID YOU KNOW?
Tuxedos don't come only in black. Today's designers have embraced midnight blue and chocolate brown as strong options for black-tie dressing.

TUXEDOS COME IN ONE-, TWO-, AND THREE-BUTTON STYLES, AND ARE EITHER SINGLE- OR DOUBLE-BREASTED, JUST LIKE SUIT JACKETS AND SPORT COATS. WHEN CHOOSING FORMAL WEAR, OPT FOR WHICHEVER NUMBER OF BUTTONS SUITS YOU BEST IN YOUR EVERYDAY LIFE.

Single-breasted tuxedo jackets are straightforward and easy to wear. Double-breasted, with two rows of buttons, can be tricky to put on—and to pull off. While the double-breasted jacket has become less popular than it used to be, fans of the style needn't worry.

The shawl collar is a design element unique to the tuxedo—it's virtually impossible to find a shawl-collared suit. The shawl collar is a lapel that folds over, forming an unbroken curve across the shoulders and ending at the jacket's button. Its elegance is timeless.

Read on to check out your options for accessorizing.

DID YOU KNOW?
The first tuxedo was worn by Pierre Lorillard at a formal ball in 1886 in Tuxedo Park, NY.

how to wear

STUDS

Coordinating with cuff links, these fancy little buttons are like jewelry for your shirt.

WING COLLAR

The classic stand-up collar looks best with an elegant bow tie.

SHOES

Probably your only opportunity to wear black patent leather and still be considered conservative.

PLAIN FRONT

Just like the pants of the same name: No pleats here.

SOCKS

Formal black socks are required for a formal shoe.

VEST

An alternative to the cummerbund, a vest is a great place to inject some texture and pattern.

CUFF LINKS

Coordinated with studs, they're a subtle way to express your personal style.

BOW TIE

Black is traditional, but there are a myriad of fabric options.

POCKET SQUARE

Another way to layer on luxe texture.

BRACES

Because you don't want to wear your everyday belt.

LIE-DOWN COLLAR

Its points face downward, giving it a similar look to that of a point collar.

TIE

Just because it's black-tie doesn't mean it's bow tie.

SCARF

Has the timelessness of a great black-and-white movie.

PLEATED FRONT

A series of folds create a decorative bib on the front of the shirt.

CUMMERBUND

A thick band of fabric that wraps around the waist.

STREAMLINED ELEGANCE

MODERN MONOCHROMATIC

Are there any rules I need to know when wearing a tuxedo?
Never cuff a tuxedo trouser. Always wear your cummerbund pleats pointing up—it's said that their original purpose was to catch crumbs. Never wear a matching bow tie, cummerbund, and pocket square—this screams "rental!" Always wear a formal black shoe or a high-shine leather lace-up (but never a worn-in business shoe).

When should I wear a white dinner jacket?
Think of a white dinner jacket as a (really) fancy blazer. Once you have a tuxedo in your wardrobe, the white dinner jacket in tropical-weight worsted wool is a good warm-weather option for both serious and casual events. You can wear it casually with an open-collar shirt, or make it formal, old-Hollywood style, with a bow tie.

How do I wear a vest?
Look on a vest as you do a necktie; it's an accessorizing option that allows you to change the look of the tux you've invested in. It can make you stand out in the sea of tuxedos at a traditional black-tie function. Choose a vest with a subtle texture or a pattern that intrigues you—maybe a stripe, a paisley, or a foulard. Stay away from "conversational" patterns inspired by themes—hopefully you'll have enough things besides your vest to discuss at the event.

How can I make my tuxedo my own?
Formal wear is deliberate. Don't be lazy; incorporate elements of your personal history—your grandfather's watch, your dad's bow tie—into your look.

RESOURCES

THE MORE YOU KNOW, THE BETTER OFF YOUR WARDROBE WILL BE. FROM INTERNATIONAL SIZING TO CARE LABELS, CLOSET ORGANIZATION TO PACKING TIPS, WE'VE GATHERED AND SIMPLIFIED A WEALTH OF HELPFUL INFORMATION. DON'T WORRY, WE WON'T QUIZ YOU LATER—FEEL FREE TO COME BACK TO THIS CHAPTER AGAIN AND AGAIN.

SIZES CAN BE HARD TO DECIPHER, SINCE THEIR SYSTEMS VARY FROM COUNTRY TO COUNTRY.

MEN'S SUIT SIZES

 🇺🇸🇬🇧	34R	36R	38R	40R	42R	44R	46R	48R
 🇪🇺	44	46	48	50	52	54	56	58

MEN'S SHIRT SIZES

 🇺🇸🇬🇧	14	14.5	15	15.5	16	16.5	17	17.5	18	18.5	19
 🇪🇺	36	37	38	39	40	41	42	43	44	45	46

MEN'S PANT SIZES

 🇺🇸	30	32	34	36	38	40
 🇬🇧	46	48	52	54	56	58
 🇪🇺	46	48	50	52	54	56

SUITS/JACKETS: To convert a European size to a U.S. size, subtract 10
(Example: European 48 = 38 Regular)

PANTS: To convert a European size to a U.S. size, subtract 16
(Example: European 46 = 30 Waist)

CARE LABELS ARE DIFFICULT TO MAKE SENSE OF—EVEN IF THEY ARE
SIMPLE LINE DRAWINGS! HERE'S WHAT THE SYMBOLS STAND FOR:

MACHINE WASH
This symbol indicates that a garment may
be cleaned to remove soil through the use
of water, detergent, and agitation. If no
temperature is given, cold water can be
used on a regular basis.

| Machine Wash | Cold Wash | Gentle Wash | Hot Wash |

TUMBLE DRY
If no temperature setting is listed, a safe
bet is medium heat. Exceptions are shown.

| Normal Dry | Low Heat | Do Not Tumble Dry | Tumble Dry No Heat | Dry Flat |

IRON
This symbol indicates that the garment needs
ironing on a regular basis. Again, there are
exceptions (see right). Spray starch is fine
if used sparingly, but it can make garments
brittle over time.

| Iron | Do Not Iron | No Steam | Iron Low |

DRY CLEAN
If a label says "dry clean," all pieces of the
garment, including the outer shell, lining,
buttons, interfacing, fusing material, and trim,
can withstand the dry-cleaning process
and will not be altered during cleaning.
Any exceptions can be determined by a
dry-cleaning professional.

| Do Not Dry Clean | Dry Clean |

DID YOU KNOW?
You should dry clean your suits after five or six wearings.

YOU SHOULD ENJOY "SHOPPING" IN YOUR CLOSET AS MUCH AS IN YOUR FAVORITE STORE. HERE'S WHAT TO DO TO MAKE YOUR CLOSET WORK FOR YOU.

ORGANIZING YOUR CLOSET

Place things in the order you put them on.

Start by hanging your shirts to the far left of your closet, beginning with solid and basic and moving to fancy and colorful.

Next, hang your trousers—by their hems, on clip hangers.

Follow with sport coats, then suits, then belts and ties.

TIPS

• Keep tissue between folded items to protect them.

• Shoe trees will help your shoes keep their shape. Both plastic and cedar ones work well for this purpose, but cedar will also absorb moisture and leave a fresh scent.

• Rotate your shoes and polish them after every third wearing.

• Use cedar blocks or chips to keep your closet smelling fresh.

WHAT YOU NEED:

5 suits

5 sport coats

5 trousers (dress)

3 pants (casual)

15 shirts

10 ties

4 pairs of shoes:
　　　　lace-up
　　　　loafer
　　　　boot
　　　　canvas

4 belts (that complement the shoes above)

Socks, underwear, T-shirts

4 pairs of jeans:
　　　　black
　　　　dark blue
　　　　washed
　　　　lived-in

Tuxedo and accoutrements

10 pieces of knitwear:
　　　　3 crew necks
　　　　3 V-necks
　　　　2 vests
　　　　2 cardigans

5 fun sport shirts

5 great T-shirts

MANY OF US ARE SO INTIMIDATED BY STAINS THAT WE'D SOONER BUY A NEW PIECE OF CLOTHING THAN TRY TO REMOVE THEM. AS WITH MOST THINGS, THE KEY WITH STAINS IS TO WORK SMART, NOT HARD. CONSULT THE LIST BELOW TO LEARN HOW TO REMOVE SPECIFIC SUBSTANCES—YOU MAY BE SURPRISED BY SOME OF THE TRICKS.

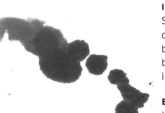

INK
Spray heavily with hair spray or douse with rubbing alcohol and blot. Sponge on detergent before dropping the garment into the washer.

BLOOD
Hold the fabric under cool, running water while rubbing it against itself. Avoid hot water, which will only set the stain permanently.

OILS
Blot excess oil with a cloth or napkin. Work baking soda or cornstarch into the stain to draw it out. Wash with detergent.

KETCHUP
Scrape off any excess and then apply a mixture of cool water and liquid dish soap (or hand soap). For heavier stains, blot with white vinegar.

PERSPIRATION
Saturate the area with shampoo—preferably one for normal hair, as shampoos for dry hair can contain too many conditioners—and then launder the garment as usual.

RED WINE
Blot with club soda. The salt helps prevent permanent staining while the bubbles in the soda help lift the stain.

COFFEE/TEA
Rinse with white vinegar or commercial stain remover. Blot.

GRASS
Soak the area in white vinegar for one hour, then wash.

CHOCOLATE
Scrape off most of the stain with a dull knife or spoon. Then saturate the spot with a solution made from a tablespoon of an enzyme detergent, like Wisk, and two cups of water. Let stand for twenty minutes, then rinse thoroughly.

LIPSTICK
Remove as much as possible with a credit card or dull knife. Dab with baby wipes, then rinse with hot water to dissolve the oils.

CHEWING GUM
Freeze the gum with a wrapped ice cube, then peel it off the garment.

USUALLY I CHOOSE TO LEAVE THE PRESSING TO THE DRY CLEANER, BUT ARMED WITH THE RIGHT INFORMATION AND A GOOD IRON, ANY MAN CAN SAVE TIME AND MONEY BY TAKING WRINKLES INTO HIS OWN HANDS. HERE'S HOW:

BEFORE YOU START

Fill your iron with cool, clean water. If your tap water is hard, you may want to use distilled water in order to keep mineral deposits from forming on the iron.

Make sure your iron is set to the proper temperature for the fabric of your shirt. Check the label if you're not sure what your shirt is made of. Temperature is key to success—too cool and the iron won't remove creases; too hot, and the iron can scorch fabric.

Prepare the fabric. If the shirt is deeply wrinkled, spray it lightly with water from a spray bottle.

Turn on the iron's steam function.

Iron the shirt in the order shown at right.

TIPS

Use the pointed tip of the iron to get into tight spaces and around button holes.

Use spray starch on areas where you want extra crispness, such as the collar and cuffs. But don't use too much on the body of the shirt—overstarched shirts can actually wrinkle more easily.

Immediately after you finish, hang the shirt and let it cool. The fabric can wrinkle easily while it's hot.

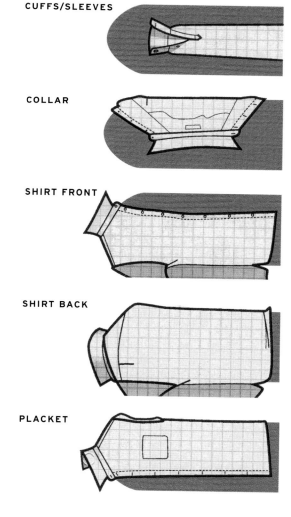

CUFFS/SLEEVES

COLLAR

SHIRT FRONT

SHIRT BACK

PLACKET

PACKING WELL MAY SEEM LIKE AN ART, BUT IT'S REALLY A CRAFT—THE MORE YOU DO IT, THE BETTER AT IT YOU'LL BECOME. YOU SHOULD KEEP TWO GOALS IN MIND WHEN PACKING FOR A TRIP: MAXIMIZING SPACE AND MINIMIZING WRINKLING. HERE ARE SUREFIRE STRATEGIES FOR ARRIVING IN STYLE.

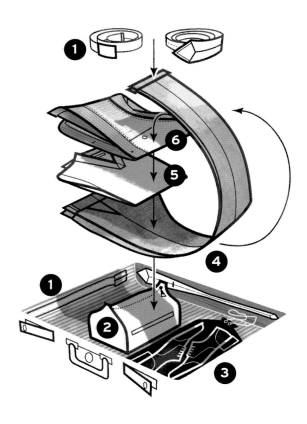

1 **BELTS & TIES** can be rolled into disks and placed on top of clothes after packing, or lie straight along the inner circumference of your suitcase.

2 **PACK HEAVY & BULKY ITEMS** on the bottom of your suitcase. Your toiletry kit will be most stable there, but be sure to wrap containers filled with liquids in plastic bags so they don't leak all over your clothes when cabin pressure changes. And remember to keep a toothbrush in your carry-on bag.

3 **SHOES** should be placed in shoe bags and can be stuffed with socks to save space.

4 **TO PACK PANTS** Fold at the crease and drape lengthwise in your suitcase, with the legs hanging over one end. Add a layer of tissue or plastic, then pile your shirts and sweaters on top of the pants (this softens the fold and prevents a deep crease). Finally, fold the pant legs back over the shirts and sweaters, creating an envelope effect. Tissue allows clothes to slide, not rub, which prevents wrinkling.

⑤ FOLD SWEATERS & SHIRTS as shown, and then fold in thirds horizontally so that the tail, the center of the garment, and then the collar area are at the top. Stack sweaters and shirts so that collar areas are face-to-face and alternate top to bottom.

⑥ FOLDING A SUIT JACKET If you are not able to hang your suit jacket or sport coat for traveling, see the diagram to the right.

1. Turn the jacket inside out (except the sleeves), so that if something spills, you can easily replace the lining.

2. Fold the jacket vertically down its back so that its front is showing.

3. Fold the jacket in half horizontally.

⑦ BRING A COLLAPSIBLE TOTE for laundry or purchases made on the road.

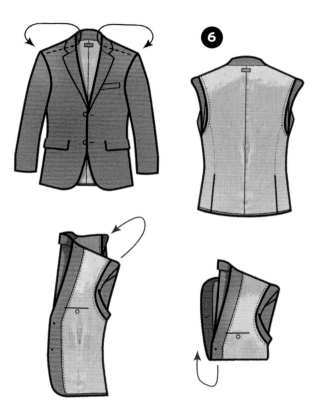

HOW TO PACK A GARMENT BAG

1. Hang a shirt and tie on one hanger.

2. Hang the suit on a separate hanger, then drape it over the hanger holding the shirt and tie. Place a plastic dry-cleaning bag over the whole thing to prevent wrinkling.

3. Place shoes, socks, and belt in the bottom of the garment bag.

NORDSTROM SERVICES

ON-SITE TAILORING AND ALTERATIONS
Receive complimentary alterations on most full-price apparel items purchased in store or at nordstrom.com.

MADE-TO-ORDER DRESS SHIRTS AND TIES
Nordstrom crafts their made-to-order John W. Nordstrom dress shirts and ties for a personalized fit. Each shirt is made from Egyptian Giza two-ply cotton and fits your individual measurements. Choose between three fits, as many as eighty-five fabrics, and 130 neck and sleeve combinations. Custom-made neckwear comes in an array of fabrics, patterns are masterfully matched, and the workmanship is signature Nordstrom. Selected stores.

MADE-TO-MEASURE SUITS
A custom-tailored suit is the ultimate investment in quality and style. You choose the fabric, style, and cut. A Nordstrom salesperson will take your measurements and have your suit made by Armani Collezioni, Burberry, Hart Schaffner Marx, Hickey Freeman, Joseph Abboud, or Ermenegildo Zegna. Selected stores.

COMPLIMENTARY PERSONAL STYLISTS
A Nordstrom personal stylist can help you with everything from buying a gift to putting together an entire wardrobe—they'll even do your shopping for you. Ask for a personal stylist at selected Nordstrom stores.

CERTIFIED SHOE FITTERS
Every Nordstrom salesperson is specially trained to ensure you receive a perfect fit. An array of selected brands are also available in extended sizes.

SHOESHINE STAND
Located in the Men's Shoes department. Selected stores.

EXTENDED SIZES
Pants, jackets, dress shirts, shoes, and more—you'll find an outstanding selection of sizes to ensure an exceptional fit. At selected Nordstrom stores and at nordstrom.com.

BUY ONLINE, PICK UP IN STORE
It's the most convenient way to fit wardrobing into your busy schedule. Just go to nordstrom.com and choose from selected items that can be shipped to your door or picked up at your nearest Nordstrom store during business hours.

THREE WAYS TO SHOP

RING US
Call 1.800.933.3365;
for TTY service for the deaf and hard
of hearing, call 1.800.685.2100.

CLICK HERE
Shop online 24/7
at nordstrom.com.

STOP BY
Simply visit your favorite
Nordstrom store.